The 241st
Royal Academy of Arts
Summer Exhibition

8 June – 16 August 2009

LIST OF WORKS

Compiled by Alice Bygraves, Chris Cook, Edith Devaney,
    Lorna Dryden, Laura Egan, Kay Harwood and Paul Sirr

Production by Abbie Coppard, Sally Goble and
    Carola Krueger
Designed by 01.02
Printed by Trade Winds

Published by RA Publications
Royal Academy of Arts
Piccadilly
London W1J 0BD

Contents

Sponsor's preface

Insight Investment is delighted, as lead sponsor, to continue its association with the Royal Academy of Arts and the artistic talent for which the Summer Exhibition is widely renowned.

Insight is a specialist asset manager at the forefront of building investment solutions designed specifically to meet its clients' evolving needs. Launched in 2002, we have grown to become one of the largest asset managers in the UK, winning industry recognition for our investment capabilities. Our investment platform has been built to give complete flexibility across a broad range of asset classes, an essential tool in providing tailored client solutions. With well-resourced, highly skilled teams, we aim to achieve consistent and repeatable returns. We cover the entire risk/return spectrum, offering our clients absolute or relative return performance benchmarks.

Our ongoing partnership with the Royal Academy is driven by two shared values: innovation and creative thinking. Innovation is key to the development of our investment capabilities and as leaders in our particular areas of expertise we continue to look for opportunities to expand our business to reach new clients and countries. For us, creative thinking is about breaking ground, challenging convention and thinking boldly and differently in everything we do, qualities that are in abundance at this year's Summer Exhibition.

This is now our fourth year of sponsorship and we very much hope that visitors to the exhibition, along with our clients, business partners and colleagues, will find new sources of inspiration in the works on display.

More insight. Not more of the same.

Managing Director

Insight
INVESTMENT

Royal Academy of Arts in London, 2009

Registered Charity No. 212798

Awards and prizes

A total of over £65,000 is offered in awards and prizes for every category of work in the Summer Exhibition:

The Royal Academy of Arts Charles Wollaston Award
£25,000 to be awarded by a panel of judges appointed by the President and Council for the most distinguished work in the exhibition.

Bovis Lend Lease and the Architects' Journal Awards for Architecture
£15,000 donated by Bovis Lend Lease and the Architects' Journal: £10,000 for a project, yet to be constructed, that communicates through its presentation most effectively both to members of the profession and the general public; £5,000 for the best work by a first-time exhibitor in the Summer Exhibition.

The Jack Goldhill Award for Sculpture
£10,000 for a sculpture.

The Hugh Casson Drawing Prize
£5,000 for an original work on paper in any medium, where the emphasis is clearly on drawing.

The Sunny Dupree Family Award
£3,500 for a painting or sculpture.

The London Original Print Fair Prize
£2,000 for a print in any medium.

The British Institution Awards
Four prizes of £1,000 each are awarded by the Trustees of the British Institution for Promoting the Fine Arts in the United Kingdom, which was established in 1805 to encourage the study of the fine arts. Students entering paintings, works on paper, sculpture and architecture will be eligible for the awards.

The Worshipful Company of Chartered Architects Award
£1,300 donated by the Worshipful Company of Chartered Architects for a drawing (or set of drawings) of a work of architecture. This may be of any age or style and any medium can be used.

The Rose Award for Photography
£1,000 for a photograph or series of photographs

Submission and sale of works

The Summer Exhibition	The Royal Academy's Summer Exhibition is the largest open contemporary art exhibition in the world, drawing together a wide range of new work by both established and unknown living artists. Held annually since the Royal Academy's foundation in 1768, the Summer Exhibition is a unique showcase for art of all styles and media, encompassing paintings, sculpture, prints and architectural models. An essential part of the London art calendar, the show draws over 150,000 visitors during its three-month run. Some 1,200 works are included and, following long Academy tradition, the exhibition is curated by an annually rotating committee whose members are all practising artists. The majority of works are for sale. Any artist may enter work for selection.
Entering works	An artist is entitled to submit a maximum of two works. If you are interested in entering work for next year's Summer Exhibition, details may be obtained from the Royal Academy's website, www.royalacademy.org.uk, from January 2010. Alternatively, please send a C5-sized stamped, addressed envelope to the Summer Exhibition Office, Royal Academy of Arts, Burlington House, Piccadilly, London WIJ 0BD.
Sales of works	All prices are inclusive of VAT where applicable. Sold works are marked with red spots. The Royal Academy levies a commission of 30% (plus VAT) on sales. A deposit equal to the commission will be taken by the Academy when the offer to purchase is registered. Cheques, credit cards and cash are all acceptable. Upon notification by the Academy, the artist will contact the intending purchaser to formally accept the offer and request the balance of payment. If for any reason the artist does not accept the offer, the commission will be returned to the purchaser by the Academy.
Editions coming from abroad	Please be aware that purchasing editions by artists who live abroad may incur extra transportation/importation costs, and in this event these costs must be met by the purchaser. All artists' addresses are listed in the back of this book and are printed on the Offer to Purchase.

Collection of purchased works	All exhibited works must remain on display until the exhibition closes. Towards the close of the exhibition, the artist, having received the balance of payment from the intending purchaser, will forward a signed Removal Order to the purchaser. The purchaser may collect the work from the Royal Academy on production of this card between Saturday 22 August and Friday 18 September 2009, Monday to Friday between 8 am and 5 pm, Saturday between 9 am and 4 pm. Collection cannot be made on Sundays or on Monday 31 August (bank holiday).

The artist will send unframed editions of prints directly to the purchaser once the artist has received the balance of payment. |
| **Intellectual property rights** | Under the Copyright, Designs and Patents Act 1988, it is the general rule that, in the absence of any agreement to the contrary, copyright in a work of art belongs to the artist, or his or her heirs and assigns. The artist also enjoys certain moral rights for the term of copyright, i.e. the rights of paternity and integrity. |
| **Academy Framing offer** | As a special offer, prints purchased from the Summer Exhibition will be framed, on production of the sales receipt, at a 15% discount on the normal cost of framing. |

Current and future exhibitions

ROBERT AUSTIN RA
Prints and Drawings
Tennant Room
Until 25 October 2009
Free admission

HIGH ART
Reynolds and History Painting 1780–1815
The John Madejski Fine Rooms
Until 29 November 2009
Free admission

HIGH LIFE
Celebrating the Loan of W. P. Frith's *Private View* *at the Royal Academy*, 1881
The John Madejski Fine Rooms
Until 29 November 2009
Free admission

J. W. WATERHOUSE
The Modern Pre-Raphaelite
The Sackler Wing of Galleries
27 June – 13 September 2009

ANISH KAPOOR
Main Galleries
26 September – 11 December 2009

WILD THING
Epstein, Gaudier-Brzeska, Gill
The Sackler Wing of Galleries
24 October 2009 – 24 January 2010

CATALOGUE

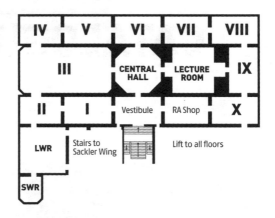

The Courtyard The Annenberg Courtyard
I Harry & Carol Djanogly Gallery
II Harry & Carol Djanogly Gallery
LWR Large Weston Room
SWR Small Weston Room
III The American Associates Gallery
IV
V The Jeanne Kahn Gallery
VI The Philip and Pauline Harris Gallery
Central Hall The Wohl Central Hall
VII The John Madejski Gallery
VIII The Weldon Gallery
IX The John A. Roberts FRIBA Gallery
Lecture Room
X The Porter Gallery

(cloakrooms are situated on the ground floor)

COURTYARD

1 TRITON III *
stainless steel
Bryan Kneale RA

2 WHY ME *acrylic* John Wragg RA	£ 5,000

---

2 WHY ME £ 5,000
acrylic
John Wragg RA

---

3 INCIDENT £ 5,000
acrylic
John Wragg RA

---

4 DOUBLE TAKE, GRAND CENTRAL II £ 59,850
oil
Bill Jacklin RA

---

5 K. 17 PROTOGEN RPT WITH TRANSPARENT TUSK £ 220,500
INFILL (MID-SIZE)
protogen rpt with transparant tusk infill and
stainless steel
Frank Stella Hon RA

---

6 TRYPTIQUE NFS
mixed media
Anselm Kiefer Hon RA

---

7 K. 37 LATTICE VARIATION PROTOGEN RPT £ 220,500
(MID-SIZE)
protogen rpt with stainless steel tubing
Frank Stella Hon RA

---

8 LENIN IM LEHNSTUHL *
oil
Georg Baselitz Hon RA

---

9 WINTER TIGER, 26-10-06 NFS
acrylic on cotton
John Hoyland RA

---

* Refer to Sales Desk

10 SILVER LAKE OPERATIONS #13 LAKE LEFROY, WESTERN AUSTRALIA £ 15,500
chromogenic colour print
Edward Burtynsky
(edition of 6: £14,500 each)

11 AIXETA / TAP £ 179,000
mixed media and assemblage on wood
Antoni Tàpies Hon RA

12 MEDITERRANEO £ 115,000
oil
Mimmo Paladino Hon RA

13 OAKWOOD 'PICCADILLY'S PECCADILLOES' £ 6,000
c-print photograph
Rut Blees Luxemborg
(edition of 5: £6,000 each)

14 SPLIT INFINITIVE 7 £ 3,250
acrylic
Flavia Irwin RA

15 UNTITLED (1996) £ 4,500
charcoal on paper
Sir Anthony Caro RA

16 LES METAMORPHOSES DU JOUR 1 £ 1,495
from a set of twelve woodcuts
Mimmo Paladino Hon RA
(edition of 30: £1,495 each)

17 LES METAMORPHOSES DU JOUR 2 £ 1,495
from a series of twelve woodcuts
Mimmo Paladino Hon RA
(edition of 30: £1,495 each)

18 LES METAMORPHOSES DU JOUR 3 £ 1,495
from a series of twelve woodcuts
Mimmo Paladino Hon RA
(edition of 30: £1,495 each)

19 UNTITLED (1996) £ 4,500
charcoal on paper
Sir Anthony Caro RA

20 ENVY £ 4,778
from a series of seven screenprints
Michael Craig-Martin RA
(edition of 30: £3,738 each)

21 BLAZING ORIFICES NFS
acrylic
Ed Ruscha Hon RA

22 REBUNDANCE £ 690,000
fire wax and transfer on canvas
The Late Robert Rauschenberg Hon RA

23 COME DANCING £ 16,100
oil
Allen Jones RA

24 SUNBURST, 2009 £ 12,000
oil
Frederick Gore RA

25 TUMBLE £ 80,500
oil
Allen Jones RA

26 ENCHANTERESSE £ 74,000
bronze, mixed media figure with stainless steel base
Allen Jones RA
(edition of 8: £74,000 each)

27 TOWER *
acrylic and charcoal on canvas
Tony Bevan RA

28 HEAD HORIZON *
acrylic and charcoal on canvas
Tony Bevan RA

29 THE OWL AND THE PUSSYCAT WENT TO SEA £ 23,000
oil
Gillian Ayres RA

30 LOST AND FOUND £ 1,950
acrylic
Mali Morris

31 AFTER THE RAIN £ 1,100
oil and wax on canvas
Philippa Stjernsward

32 INDECISIVE ACCEPTANCE £ 1,000
linen cloth, paper clay, arylic and oil paint
Noriko Watanabe

33 HARVEST £ 1,100
oil and wax on canvas
Philippa Stjernsward

34 UNCOVERED £ 1,950
acrylic
Mali Morris

35 SHADWELL, 2006 £ 20,700
acrylic
Albert Irvin RA

* Refer to Sales Desk

36 DRAWING 1487 (DIPTYCH) £ 16,525
gouache and charcoal on paper
Nigel Hall RA

37 POLAR MELT 2009 £ 18,000
encaustic wax and beach detritus on styrofoam
Terry Setch

38 NO KNOWN WAY (JANUS SERIES) £ 21,850
oil and wax
Basil Beattie RA

39 THE SIGHT OF NIGHT I (JANUS SERIES) £ 21,850
oil and wax
Basil Beattie RA

40 AT FIRST LIGHT (OXFORD) £ 11,500
polished wood
Nigel Hall RA

41 MUTATIS MUTANDIS XIV £ 17,825
acrylic
Paul Huxley RA

42 MUTATIS MUTANDIS XV £ 17,825
acrylic
Paul Huxley RA

43 LOST IN BLUE, 24-12-08 NFS
acrylic on cotton
John Hoyland RA

44 UNTITLED *
acrylic on aluminium
Michael Craig-Martin RA

45 CLARITAS (CLOUD AND SKY), 2009 £ 6,000
oil and acrylic on canvas
Gretchen Albrecht

46 YELLOW/GREEN/RED (INTERIOR WITH £ 3,000
RED FLOOR), 2008
oil on 3 panels with toughened glass
James Ross

* Refer to Sales Desk

47 AFTER DAMASCUS £ 14,000
mixed media
Tess Jaray

48 GREEK HORSE £ 97,750
bronze
William Tucker RA
(edition of 6)

49 SONG SCHOOL £ 15,000
bronze
Paul De Monchaux
(edition of 7: £15,000 each)

50 WITTGENSTEIN'S DILEMMA II £ 48,000
steel
Tom Phillips RA

LARGE WESTON ROOM

51 AUTUMN LOVE I (PINK LOUNGE) £ 941
etching and inkjet
Anthony Green RA
(edition of 20: £863 each)

52 DOWN TO THE WOODS £ 550
lithograph
Jessie Brennan
(edition of 10: £450 each)

53 STUDIO £ 978
woodcut
Arturo Di Stefano
(edition of 15: £863 each)

54 MIRROR POND £ 850
woodcut
Nana Shiomi
(edition of 30: £620 each)

55 WINTER ALMONDS £ 1,177
screenprint
Barbara Rae RA
(edition of 125: £975 each)

56 SANCTUARY £ 890
woodcut
Nana Shiomi
(edition of 30: £620 each)

57 ON LINE I £ 375
etching
Vanessa Jackson
(edition of 25: £300 each)

58 ON LINE II £ 375
etching
Vanessa Jackson
(edition of 25: £300 each)

59 WORDS AND DEEDS 2009 £ 1,050
screenprint
Stephen Chambers RA
(edition of 30: £800 each)

60 MORAR £ 650
screenprint
John Mackechnie
(edition of 25: £550 each)

61 BOX JUNCTION £ 250
silkscreen on Somerset stain 300gsm
Mathew Sant
(edition of 30: £135 each)

62 O'RAMANATHA £ 950
etching
Christopher Roantree
(edition of 10: £850 each)

63 DANCER RESTING £ 4,000
drawing over ink on copper plate monoprint
Leonard McComb RA

64 PROMISED LAND £ 495
etching and archival digital print
Barton Hargreaves
(edition of 25: £400 each)

65 INCOMING £ 450
etching and aquatint
Sara Lee
(edition of 25: £350 each)

66 MEANWHILE £ 350
etching and aquatint
Sara Lee
(edition of 25: £280 each)

67 SHEAR DESCENT £ 850
etching, aquatint, chine collé mounted on linen
Matthew Coombes
(edition of 5: £700 each)

68 BLOSSFELDT... AFTER BLOSSFELDT – ART FORMS £ 3,466
IN NATURE
lithograph
Idris Khan
(edition of 40: £3,060 each)

69 BLUE MUSIC £ 375
lithograph
Alan Cox
(edition of 25: £330 each)

70 PORTRAIT OF GEMMA £ 4,000
monoprint
Leonard McComb RA

71 ONES COMPANY 2009 £ 1,050
screenprint
Stephen Chambers RA
(edition of 30: £800 each)

72 SPUN FAN £ 500
etching
Farah Syed
(edition of 15: £400 each)

73 DEPRESSED NOISE £ 850
etching, aquatint, chine collé, mounted on linen
Matthew Coombes
(edition of 5: £700 each)

74 THE GAME £ 425
silkscreen
Inge Borg Scott
(edition of 35: £375 each)

75 A FIDDLE £ 995
hand constructed, digitally printed paper and glue
Ceal Warnants
(edition of 2: £995 each)

76 SUDARIUM OF NEUKÖLLN £ 7,000
Unique screenprint
Lee Wagstaff

77 GUARDIANS £ 2,473
etching and aquatints
Paula Rego
(edition of 35: £2,350 each)

78 STEERING THE BOAT, 2009 £ 2,553
etching and aquatint
Paula Rego
(edition of 35: £2,300 each)

79 28 NFS
woodcut on paper
Katsutoshi Yuasa
(edition of 5)

80 LITTLE DARLING £ 575
woodcut
Eileen Cooper RA
(edition of 40: £500 each)

81 GIRL HOLDING RABBIT £ 225
etching
Leonard McComb RA
(edition of 50: £190 each)

82 MIDSUMMER BUTTERFLY £ 150
photo etching
Emma McCarthy
(edition of 20: £110 each)

83 BLACK DOG AT TOWER BRIDGE £ 825
paper cut relief
Chris Orr RA
(edition of 30: £700 each)

84 EDEN, ARK AND EVOLUTION £ 775
etching with hand colouring
Chris Orr RA
(edition of 30: £650 each)

85 ECHOES   NFS
woodcut on paper
Katsutoshi Yuasa
(edition of 5)

86 WEST SIDE STORY, FROM THE CHELSEA HOTEL   £ 1,050
relief etching with hand colouring
Chris Orr RA
(edition of 25: £850 each)

87 CROSS THIS BRIDGE WHEN YOU COME TO IT, BROOKLYN NEW YORK   £ 1,050
etching chine collé and paper cut relief
Chris Orr RA
(edition of 25: £850 each)

88 CROSSCURRENT   £ 1,090
woodcut
Eileen Cooper RA
(edition of 15: £900 each)

89 OUR WORLDS COLLIDED   £ 900
screenprint on paper
Leigh Clarke
(edition of 25: £550 each)

90 FELDER   £ 2,863
woodcut on kozo paper
Christiane Baumgartner
(edition of 12: £2,415 each)

91 PLANTAGE   £ 2,863
woodcut on kozo paper
Christiane Baumgartner
(edition of 12: £2,415 each)

92 THE BLIND HOUSE 5   £ 600
etching
Moyna Flannigan
(edition of 30: £500 each)

93 THE BLIND HOUSE 1   £ 600
etching
Moyna Flannigan
(edition of 30: £500 each)

94 UNTITLED (IT REALLY DOESN'T MATTER AT ALL) £ 720
coloured pencil and pen
Elizabeth Collini

95 POSTCARD FROM HEAVEN £ 1.99
printed card
Ali Eisa

96 PRINT, 2007 £ 300
ink on paper
Michael Landy RA
(edition of 150)

97 I'VE ALWAYS BEEN IN LOVE WITH YOU £ 1,550
mixed media multiple
Sue Whale
(edition of 25: £1,550 each)

98 WOODCUTTER'S WOOD £ 595
woodcut
Richard Wincer
(edition of 30: £475 each)

99 CRUCIFIXION AND MOUNTAIN £ 2,475
screenprint
Craigie Aitchison RA
(edition of 75: £1,725 each)

100 EVER CHANGING SKY LINE £ 450
sugar lift etching
Simon Lawson
(edition of 25: £300 each)

101 LAMBETH £ 875
etching
Chris Orr RA
(edition of 40: £750 each)

102 CREST £ 700
archival inkjet
Bryan Kneale RA
(edition of 20: £590 each)

103 DARK BALTIC TRADER £ 335
wood and lithography
Francis Tinsley
(edition of 50: £255 each)

104 NEW EMPIRE (DOUBLE ARAUCARIA ARAUCANA) £ 490
photo etching
Andrew Curtis
(edition of 10: £400 each)

105 CARRADALE £ 650
screenprint
John Mackechnie
(edition of 20: £550 each)

106 PUEBLO £ 1,177
silkscreen
Barbara Rae RA
(edition of 125: £975 each)

107 THE BLASKET ISLANDS £ 500
etching
Norman Ackroyd RA
(edition of 90: £350 each)

108 SWAMP HOODIE, 2008 £ 750
screenprint and archival ink jet
Stephen Walter
(edition of 50: £635 each)

109 ALTER £ 850
lithograph and screenprint
Bob Matthews
(edition of 10: £700 each)

110 AQUEOUS IV £ 490
screenprint
Hetty Haxworth
(edition of 20: £420 each)

111 AN CEO DRAOCHTA £ 1,700
collagraph, etching
Barbara Rae RA
(edition of 30: £1,500 each)

112 SYBIL HEAD – CO KERRY £ 300
etching
Norman Ackroyd RA
(edition of 150: £200 each)

113 THE CLIFFS OF MOHER £ 400
etching
Norman Ackroyd RA
(edition of 90: £300 each)

114 FROM SUTTON BANK – VALE OF YORK £ 800
etching
Norman Ackroyd RA
(edition of 90: £600 each)

115 FROM MALIN HEAD – TORY ISLAND £ 500
etching
Norman Ackroyd RA
(edition of 90: £350 each)

116 WEST COAST £ 400
etching
Norman Ackroyd RA
(edition of 90: £300 each)

117 CLOSE, 2007 £ 700
etching and chine collé
Tom Hammick
(edition of 25: £610 each)

118 DRY DOCK £ 299
drypoint and watercolour
Richard Spare
(edition of 90: £225 each)

119 WAITING FOR THE FERRY, FOWEY HARBOUR £ 1,050
silkscreen
Frederick Cuming RA
(edition of 75: £850 each)

120 GARDEN UNDER SNOW £ 1,050
silkscreen
Frederick Cuming RA
(edition of 75: £850 each)

121 A HUMUMENT: SCRIBE THE STORY £ 309
epson and silkscreen
Tom Phillips RA
(edition of 75: £250 each)

122 A HUMUMENT: KING KONG £ 309
epson and silkscreen
Tom Phillips RA
(edition of 75: £250 each)

123 ROOM £ 541
soft ground etching
Celia Paul
(edition of 15: £460 each)

124 INFORMATION FOR DECISION MAKING AND £ 275
AND PARTICIPATION
digital print
Rachael Champion
(edition of 20: £225 each)

125 CONTINUOUS DEFENSE, SOUTHERN CAPE £ 255
silkscreen
Mark Harris
(edition of 20: £195 each)

126 THE ITCH £ 190
etching
Jeremy Deadman
(edition of 50: £95 each)

127 WAR AND PEACE £ 2,200
ink jet print
Dick Jewell
(edition of 5: £2,000 each)

128 MEXICO £ 1,500
mixed media
Louise Clarke

129 NORTH LONDON MASCOT £ 250
silkscreen and inkjet
Oran O'Reilly
(edition of 30: £180 each)

130 NEWS BOY £ 250
silkscreen and inkjet
Oran O'Reilly
(edition of 30: £180 each)

131 NIETHER USE NOR ORNAMENT £ 4,800
oil, acrylic, inkjet on canvas
Mark Hampson

132 THIERRY HENRY £ 500
screenprint
Orlando Johnson
(edition of 20: £400 each)

133 CONSTRUCTION £ 2,000
silk on linen
Miranda Argyle

134 MOUNTAINS £ 325
screenprint
Samuel Luke Nias
(edition of 15: £280 each)

135 HIRAETHOG £ 175
linocut
Thomas Williams
(edition of 15: £155 each)

136 SPACE MONKEY £ 375
polymer gravure
Tracey Emin RA
(edition of 300: £225 each)

137 CHURCH AND STATE £ 920
inkjet and varnish
Dick Jewell
(edition of 5: £800 each)

138 STRATA, 2009 £ 220
screenprint
Roger Kelly
(edition of 100: £120 each)

139 LOST SAINT £ 280
copper plate etching
David Price
(edition of 20: £200 each)

140 THE FLOATING WORLD II £ 190
linocut
Jazmin Velasco
(edition of 100: £150 each)

141 JUNK II Editions available for sale
silk screen on arches 300 gsm
Keith Coventry
(edition of 50: £1,000 each)

142 DARWIN'S GARDEN £ 430
inkjet print, archival ink and paper
Gillian Golding
(edition of 60: £380 each)

143 WHARF STREET WEST £ 520
etching
Bronwen Sleigh
(edition of 20: £400 each)

144 ROAD WORKER AND BIRD HOUSE £ 430
etching and inkjet
Jeffrey Dennis
(edition of 5: £330 each)

145 THE LAST DANCE AT RAY'S PLACE £ 150
solar plate print
Fru Kenworthy-Browne
(edition of 50: £120 each)

146 SUDDEN GROWTH £ 215
etching
Louise Clarke
(edition of 25: £150 each)

147 INSIDE EYE £ 190
etching
Alan Smith
(edition of 45: £160 each)

148 WHARF STREET EAST £ 520
etching
Bronwen Sleigh
(edition of 20: £400 each)

149 THE EASTERN HILL STILL WALKS UPON THE WATER £ 450
woodcut and screenprint
Jason Oliver
(edition of 20: £400 each)

150 TRANSMISSION £ 450
woodcut, moku hanga, silk japanese paper
Jason Oliver
(edition of 20: £400 each)

151 OUSEBURN £ 200
wood engraving
Hilary Paynter
(edition of 100: £140 each)

152 CROSSING TO SAFETY £ 350
photo etching
Benedicte Emsens
(edition of 10: £250 each)

153 DOUBT £ 600
screenprint
Ann Hobson
(edition of 6: £450 each)

154 A POEM OF THE HARVEST III £ 880
wood block, etching
Sumiko Okubo
(edition of 35: £700 each)

155 ESTUARY £ 675
inkjet photograph
Jean Macalpine
(edition of 25: £525 each)

156 LATE SHADOWS ON THE MOUNTAINS, SICILY £ 200
(MESSINA FROM REGGIO CALABRIA)
aquatint
Peter Freeth RA
(edition of 45: £155 each)

157 DEAR SEBALD £ 320
lithograph
Michael Hall
(edition of 10: £270 each)

158 ST. IVES £ 225
wood engraving
Peter Lawrence
(edition of 40: £175 each)

159 STILL LIFE 1, 2009 £ 350
relief print
Jonathan Trayte
(edition of 13: £240 each)

160 UNTITLED £ 375
giclée print on paper
Sam Messenger
(edition of 100: £295 each)

161 FOLLOW ME £ 550
photo etching with spit bite
Simon Lawson
(edition of 25: £400 each)

162 IN THE LAND OF MILK AND HONEY £ 250
etching
Carmen Gracia
(edition of 20: £215 each)

163 PRUNING £ 4,903
*aquatint, etching, drypoint, and
mechanical abrasion*
Jim Dine
(edition of 14: £4,428 each)

164 THE RAFT £ 520
woodcut
Richard Wincer
(edition of 30: £400 each)

165 LOZENGE £ 1,150
lithograph and monoprint
Colin Gale
(edition of 15: £900 each)

166 BLACK SUN £ 450
copper plate etching
David Price
(edition of 20: £380 each)

167 I CAN CHANGE £ 2,500
silk on linen
Miranda Argyle

168 GREEN BLUES £ 690
screenprint with woodblock
Anthony Frost
(edition of 75: £460 each)

169 FROM GORKY'S DUSTBIN 3 £ 660
screenprint
Clyde Hopkins
(edition of 35: £460 each)

170 MY SPACE I £ 250
etching with carbonondrum and chine collé
Norma Silverton
(edition of 25: £200 each)

171 VENUS COLLECTION £ 450
etching
Caroline Isgar
(edition of 30: £385 each)

172 THE OLD WOMAN WHO LIVED IN A SHOE, PENELOPE – £ 400
WHAT SIZE IS YOUR SHOE? (SCENES FROM THE ODYSSEY)
lithograph with screenprint on Somerset paper
Jenny Wiener
(edition of 8: £325 each)

173 ✓✓✓!!! £ 450
etching with aquatint
Oliver Osborne
(edition of 12: £400 each)

174 BIRD STUDY, PANEL 5 £ 1,500
screenprint
Edd Pearman
(edition of 5: £1,300 each)

175 THOR HEYERDAHL £ 250
screenprint in found frame
Kasper Pincis
(edition of 16: £150 each)

176 LOLA'S THINGS £ 150
linocut
Sarah Battle
(edition of 50: £120 each)

177 TOY CAR £ 230
cardboard print
Chloe Cheese
(edition of 20: £195 each)

178 THE LITTLE OAK £ 200
woodblock
Judith Lockie
(edition of 35: £135 each)

179 PACE # 53 £ 370
etching and aquatint on Somerset paper
Holly Antrum
(edition of 10: £280 each)

180 EX NIHILO 2/15 £ 460
etching
Eleanor Havsteen-Franklin
(edition of 15: £360 each)

181 WAITING WOMAN 2008 £ 850
etching
Freya Payne
(edition of 15: £700 each)

182 LOT AND HIS DAUGHTER II £ 370
etching and aquatint
Marcelle Hanselaar
(edition of 30: £330 each)

183 MUSE £ 950
etching
Megan Fishpool
(edition of 20: £750 each)

184 10 PM £ 450
colour lithograph
Claas Gutsche
(edition of 25: £350 each)

185 WHY SO SERIOUS £ 455
mixed media print
John Miles
(edition of 75: £400 each)

186 POWER STATION, GREENWICH £ 230
lino print
Mick Armson
(edition of 20: £160 each)

187 SO HE GILDED THE TABLE £ 225
etching and gold leaf
Alexander Massouras
(edition of 60: £170 each)

188 NOVEMBER £ 400
lithocut
Claas Gutsche
(edition of 30: £300 each)

189 CONTINUOUS DEFENSE, THE BIRDS OF THE EAST, £ 450
THE BIRDS OF THE WEST
silkscreen
Mark Harris
(edition of 20: £395 each)

190 GLACIAL WATER £ 280
colour woodcut
Irmgard Parth
(edition of 25: £230 each)

191 NUBIA £ 285
etching, chine collé
Basia Lautman
(edition of 20: £215 each)

192 A JOURNEY £ 265
etching
Matthew Ablitt
(edition of 50: £165 each)

193 GOLDFISH II £ 180
mezzotint
Roger Harris
(edition of 75: £140 each)

194 LIKE A SMALL SUN £ 225
etching and gold leaf
Alexander Massouras
(edition of 60: £170 each)

195 THE LONGING £ 325
linocut print
Dean Melbourne
(edition of 25: £250 each)

196 UNDER BLACKFRIARS BRIDGE £ 245
lino print
Mick Armson
(edition of 20: £175 each)

197 FORNO PASTORALBIDONE £ 500
etching
Nicholas Hatfull
(edition of 25: £450 each)

198 BRID £ 110
stone lithograph
Mary Clark
(edition of 110: £75 each)

199 BEACHSCAPE, SUTHERLAND £ 670
screenprint
Donald Hamilton Fraser RA
(edition of 195: £495 each)

200 CROSSING THE SQUARE IN THE SNOW II £ 3,800
monotype on paper
Bill Jacklin RA

201 BEARMAN HATCHING £ 330
etching
Eem Yun Kang
(edition of 25: £230 each)

202 OXYGEN £ 285
etching
Caroline Isgar
(edition of 30: £240 each)

203 HAMPSTEAD HEATH SUMMER £ 250
drypoint and chine collé
Lucy Farley
(edition of 15: £225 each)

204 MATUKA NO.5 £ 4,750
hand painting in acrylic on paper with carborundum
printing
Gillian Ayres RA

205 SLIP £ 2,089
from a series of seven lithographs
Allen Jones RA
(edition of 50: £1,410 each)

206 ETCHED LINES: THIRTY FIVE £ 2131
etching
Ian Davenport
(edition of 25: £1,800 each)

207 THE CONVERSATION II £ 3,800
monotype on paper
Bill Jacklin RA

208 BECOMING MUSHROOM £ 330
etching
Eem Yun Kang
(edition of 25: £230 each)

209 ALBERT LOOKING AT ALBERT £ 275
etching, drypoint and chine collé
Lucy Farley
(edition of 15: £240 each)

210 STACK £ 400
relief print
Joby Williamson
(edition of 20: £330 each)

211 CHATTER £ 250
woodcut print
Michael Ward
(edition of 100: £200 each)

212 LONG DOG £ 320
woodcut
Emily Smith Polyblank
(edition of 100: £180 each)

213 AUTUMN LOVE III/ RED HOT £ 607
screenprint and inkjet
Anthony Green RA
(edition of 50: £547 each)

214 AUTUMN LOVE II/THE SWING £ 643
screenprint and inkjet
Anthony Green RA
(edition of 35: £575 each)

215 SHEPHERD'S PURSE 5, 2002 £ 1,500
etching on paper
Michael Landy RA
(edition of 37)

216 GEOMETRIC REJECTION £ 600
etching and aquatint
Ian McNicol
(edition of 7: £500 each)

217 FOOL'S PARADISE £ 400
archival digital print, screen varnish
Richard Kirwan
(edition of 30: £300 each)

218 NEBRASKA I, 2008 £ 1,100
screenprint with wood block
Albert Irvin RA
(edition of 35: £865 each)

219 NEBRASKA VIII, 2008 £ 1,100
screenprint with wood block
Albert Irvin RA
(edition of 35: £865 each)

220 THE LAST TIME £ 350
digital, silkscreen print on Somerset satin paper
Alex Knell
(edition of 15: £250 each)

221 SPORES 2 £ 1,800
handcut screenprint and woodcut construction
Fiona Hepburn

222 VIEW £ 1,200
screenprint on paper and perspex
George Charman
(edition of 10: £1,100 each)

223 WHITE RHINOCEROS £ 1,526
mezzotint
Paul Emsley
(edition of 75: £1,150 each)

224 WINTER HORSE (ANNA), OFF RIDGE LANE, DIGGLE £ 1,600
pencil
John Hewitt

225 FOUR HEADS £ 385
lithograph
Giulia Resteghini
(edition of 30: £350 each)

226 JENNY'S BASKET £ 275
etching
Jeanette Orrell
(edition of 25: £225 each)

227 COME ABOUT £ 580
silkscreen print
Eileen Cooper RA
(edition of 50: £500 each)

228 MOORING £ 580
silkscreen print
Eileen Cooper RA
(edition of 50: £500 each)

229 SPRING BULL (GALLABER BORDERWAY),   £ 1,600
OFF RIDGE LANE, DIGGLE
pencil drawing
John Hewitt

230 OPERATION X (NOVEMBER 30TH 2007)   £ 600
photo etching
Suzann Kundi
(edition of 10: £470 each)

231 LUNG CROSS SECTION   ~ £ 220
etching
Flora Parrott
(edition of 12: £180 each)

232 CHEYNE, 2008   £ 7,000
pencil on paper
Michael Landy RA

233 CAROL, 2008   £ 7,000
pencil on paper
Michael Landy RA

234 TREE-LIFE   Editions are available for sale
etching on paper
Hayoung Kim
(edition of 40: £140 each)

235 TREE-LIFE   Editions are available for sale
etching on paper
Hayoung Kim
(edition of 40: £140 each)

236 OSCAR   £ 365
etching
Helen Fay
(edition of 60: £300 each)

237 HOME I   £ 290
etching
Mila Judge-Fürstova
(edition of 35: £250 each)

238 HOME II £ 290
etching
Mila Judge–Fürstova
(edition of 35: £250 each)

239 UNFINISHED STATE £ 500
aquatint
Peter Freeth RA
(edition of 30: £425 each)

240 HEDONESTATE £ 425
aquatint etching
Frederic Morris
(edition of 18: £350 each)

241 BEACH AT GRUINARD £ 610
screenprint
Donald Hamilton Fraser RA
(edition of 130: £450 each)

242 REACH FOR THE SKY £ 450
etching
Neil Pittaway
(edition of 90: £395 each)

243 WHAT ARE LITTLE BOYS MADE OF? £ 220
etching
Martin Ridgwell
(edition of 75: £175 each)

244 CREDO: TWO (HADDON HALL) £ 400
archival inkjet and watercolour print
Jennifer Dickson RA
(edition of 20: £250 each)

245 CREDO: ONE (FOUNTAINS ABBEY) £ 400
archival inkjet and watercolour print
Jennifer Dickson RA
(edition of 20: £250 each)

246 NIGHT CITY £ 275
aquatint
Peter Freeth RA
(edition of 30: £220 each)

247 AND HE MARCHED THEM ALL DOWN AGAIN £ 525
aquatint
Peter Freeth RA
(edition of 30: £450 each)

248 FROSTY MORNING CHURCH LANE £ 300
etching, drypoint
Melvyn Petterson
(edition of 30: £250 each)

249 METROLAND £ 225
linocut
Gail Brodholt
(edition of 100: £170 each)

250 VOYAGE I £ 490
lithography print
Guler Ates
(edition of 12: £400 each)

251 CELLAR £ 850
lithograph
Nick Mobbs
(edition of 10: £750 each)

252 LAKE IV £ 3,450
monotype on paper
Bill Jacklin RA

253 SWEET THAMES, RUN SOFTLY £ 550
aquatint
Peter Freeth RA
(edition of 30: £475 each)

254 LAGOON £ 475
four colour photo etching
Suzanne Moxhay
(edition of 20: £350 each)

255 VIOLETS AND LEMON £ 285
etching and chine collé
Rachel Clark
(edition of 15: £235 each)

256 POSTCARD FROM VENICE, RUGA, 2008 £ 1,624
a set of 3 aquatints with collaged envelope
Joe Tilson RA
(edition of 30: £1,346 each)

257 LINEAR ETCHING: INTRUSION II, 2009 £ 350
etching
John Carter RA
(edition of 21: £265 each)

258 SHIMMERING LIGHT: ONE (SEATON DELAVAL) £ 625
archival inkjet and watercolour
Jennifer Dickson RA
(edition of 20: £425 each)

259 LINEAR ETCHING: INTRUSION I, 2009 £ 300
etching
John Carter RA
(edition of 21: £215 each)

260 MOSQUES £ 875
etching and watercolour
Meg Dutton
(edition of 50: £700 each)

261 POSTCARD FROM VENICE, RIO, 2008 £ 1,624
a set of 3 aquatints with collaged envelope
Joe Tilson RA
(edition of 30: £1,346 each)

262 BABY AND BUTTERFLY £ 8,400
drypoint and engraving on cloth and vintage paper
Louise Bourgeois
(edition of 15)

263 SHIMMERING LIGHT: TWO (SHUTE HOUSE) £ 500
archival inkjet and watercolour print
Jennifer Dickson RA
(edition of 40: £325 each)

264 SHIMMERING LIGHT: THREE (PALAZZO FARNESE, CAPRAROLA) £ 625
archival inkjet and watercolour print
Jennifer Dickson RA
(edition of 20: £425 each)

265 ETOILE: 4 IDENTICAL SHAPES, 2008 £ 275
blind embossing
John Carter RA
(edition of 21: £190 each)

266 LINEAR ETCHING: INTRUSION III, 2009 £ 350
etching
John Carter RA
(edition of 21: £265 each)

267 POSTCARD FROM VENICE, RIO, 2008 £ 1,624
a set of 3 aquatints with collaged envelope
Joe Tilson RA
(edition of 30: £1,346 each)

268 HOT CHERRY 2009 £ 3,200
painted bronze
Jonathan Trayte

269 RED SENTINEL £ 1,500
roofing felt
Carole Andrews

270 SUNFLOWERS £ 12,000
wood, bronze, copper
Tony Carter

271 LONGINUS LAXUS £ 17,250
fibreglass and acrylic
John Humphreys
(edition of 8: £17,250 each)

272 RAVEN £ 5,750
bronze
Dido Crosby
(edition of 12: £5,750 each)

273 SHOWTIME £ 80,500
glass reinforced plastic
Allen Jones RA
(edition of 3: £80,500 each)

274 MARATHON £ 2,100
bronze
Hylton Stockwell
(edition of 10: £2,100 each)

SMALL WESTON ROOM

275	**PONDERING** *blue ink* Leonard Manasseh RA	£ 283
276	**NOT TODAY, THANK YOU** *pastel and ink* Leonard Manasseh RA	£ 454
277	**WATCHFULL** *coloured inks* Leonard Manasseh RA	£ 295
278	**MIRAGE** *blue ink* Leonard Manasseh RA	£ 283
279	**HEAVENLY LANDSCAPE WITH SUN AND MOON** *black ink* Leonard Manasseh RA	£ 454
280	**DANCING IN RED STOCKINGS** *drawing pastel and pencil* James Butler RA	£ 1,500
281	**REES AND WILLIAMS** *watercolour* Mark Atkins	£ 3,400
282	**PANIC** *oil* Michi Araya	£ 600
283	**BLOWING A PLACE IN THE CLOUDS** *mixed media collage on paper* Emily Marbach	£ 550

284 WORLDLY GOODS £ 850
acrylic on canvas board
Michael Kennedy

285 UNTITLED £ 850
acrylic on canvas board
Michael Kennedy

286 FISHING FOR BULLHEADS £ 216
pastel
Hazel Smith

287 TENT £ 875
oil and gold leaf on board
Sophie Coryndon

288 THE WHITE HOUSE £ 395
acrylic
Lee Madgwick

289 STILL LIFE 2 £ 7,600
oil
Edmund Fairfax-Lucy

290 MATHILDA £ 2,600
oil on gesso panel
David Cooper

291 CHAIRS FOR THE ANCESTORS £ 1,000
watercolour and gouache
David Paskett

292 GRACIOUS £ 1,200
acrylic
Richard Sorrell

293 PICCADILLY CIRCUS £ 2,500
oil
Robert Hardy

294 RIPENED APPLE £ 3,350
oil on canvas on board
Charlotte Verity

295 JUG AND FLOWERS   £1,200
oil
Janet Treby

296 TWO MUSICIANS, BARCELONA   £2,800
oil
Julian Bailey

297 PLANTS AND A HAWKMOTH   £6,500
oil
Olwyn Bowey RA

298 MEASURING UP   £1,750
oil on board
Rosie Birtwhistle

299 HER THINKING SPACE   £1,300
oil
Stella Parsons

300 RUINED CHURCH   £750
arcylic on gesso
Christie Bird

301 LW   £3,500
oil on copper
Nadia Hebson

302 THE BOARDWALK BY NIGHT   £550
oil
Elizabeth Vibert

303 TOWARDS EVENING   £995
acrylic
Richard Sorrell

304 STILL LIFE: LATE AUTUMN   £7,500
oil on panel
John Morley

305 SIRENS   £1,100
oil on panel
Peter Layzell

306 THE BLUE BOWL £ 620
watercolour
Shirley Felts

307 AUNT BLAIRE'S LIVING ROOM £ 100
oil on panel
Olha Pryymak

308 THE TORN HAT (TRIBUTE TO THOMAS SULLY) £ 1,200
oil
David Payne

309 FIDO MATELOT TABLEAN £ 1,950
gouache and tempera on paper
Mick Rooney RA

310 ANNUNCIATION £ 1,900
watercolour and gold leaf on paper
Linda Sutton

311 DEATH OF A JOCKEY £ 590
oil
Sarah Rogers

312 SOPHIE £ 1,200
watercolour and pastel
James Rushton

313 ST. GIOCOMETTO, VENICE £ 895
watercolour and bodycolour
Robert Wells

314 WINTER LANDSCAPE £ 1,100
oil
Elizabeth Orchard

315 FOSSIL BEACH £ 900
watercolour pencils
Isabel Paterson

316 THE GARDEN IN WINTER £ 1,500
oil
Michael Whittlesea

317 CAPRICORN £ 900
oil on board
Simon Wright

318 WINTER ALLOTMENTS £ 890
oil
Christopher Miers

319 THE WIRE FENCE £ 950
oil
Anna Teasdale

320 THE HOSPITABLE GARDENER £ 1,750
egg tempera and oils
Marcelle Milo-Gray

321 SUNLIGHT AND THE OPEN DOOR £ 2,000
oil
Peter Kelly

322 FLIGHT OF BIRDS £ 6,500
oil
Olwyn Bowey RA

323 THE HARVEST £ 900
oil
Brian Hanson

324 TAKE ME BACK TO BLIGHTY £ 850
acrylic and egg tempera
Mick Davies

325 DOG JAM £ 95
acrylic
Susan Tindall

326 ALEXANDRA, AGED 13, ON NATANYA ROOFTOP £ 3,900
oil
Naomi Alexander

327 SQUEEZING SOMETHING YOU LOVE DEARLY TO DEATH £ 2,250
oil on board
Grant Foster

328 FLEMISH ROOFSCAPE £ 400
oil on slate
David Snelling

329 OVER THE EDGE £ 740
acrylic
John Butterworth

330 TWISTY STICK 1 £ 210
oil on flax linen
Richard Baines

331 TWISTY STICK 2 £ 210
oil on flax linen
Richard Baines

332 POGOING AT THE ROXY £ 1,977
oil on linen
George Skelcher

333 ON BOARD £ 600
pva and watercolour
John Rae

334 LLANGOLLEN CANAL £ 600
pva and watercolour
John Rae

335 DOG AND ARCHES £ 450
soft pastel
Angela A'Court

336 AUTUMN MORNING £ 685
oil
Martin Cox

337 PINK DRIFT £ 750
oil
Matthew Kolakowski

338 YELLOW SKIP £ 700
acrylic and enamel on board
Florin Catalin Ungureanu

339	**ITC007**	£ 950
	oil on gesso panel	
	Richard Baker	

340	**SECOND LIFE, AFTER HAYMAN**	£ 1,300
	oil on linen	
	Lex Thomas	

341	**SE 305 397**	£ 1,200
	oil	
	Adam Stone	

342	**OLDBURY I**	£ 600
	oil	
	Louise Balaam	

343	**UNDER BLUE SKIES**	£ 750
	embroidery thread on cotton textile	
	Willemien Downes	

344	**MAKING FRIENDS**	£ 400
	etching and hand colour	
	Sandra Millar	
	(edition of 20: £340 each)	

345	**GIRL IN FOREST**	£ 750
	ink on doll's wallpaper	
	Kerry Phippen	

346	**SOUTH KENTISH TOWN TALES, PAY HOMAGE TO TO THE LOGO**	£ 500
	oil	
	Leslie Farago	

347	**ORNAMENT-CAT**	£ 800
	oil	
	Julia Hamilton	

348	**THE SILVER HORSE**	£ 3,300
	oil	
	Zoë Moss	

349	**THE EARTH AND THE SKY WILL SWALLOW YOU**	£ 485
	stitch on linen	
	Sharon Leahy-Clark	

350 THE HAIR-CURLER TREE £ 2,100
acrylic and gouache on paper
Joseph Schneider

351 THE FOOLISH BOY NFS
oil on board
Heather Nevay

352 STILL LIFE WITH PINK AND BLACK £ 1,100
watercolour
Annie Williams

353 SLEEPER BUS, RAJASTHAN £ 2,900
oil on board
Theon Pearce

354 RIDE THE CALM MID-HEAVEN £ 255
linocut
Rebecca Hearle
(edition of 11: £155 each)

355 SEVEN LEGGED LAMB £ 160
etching
Flora Parrott
(edition of 20: £120 each)

356 WEST 10 ST DELI NY £ 275
etching
Austin Cole
(edition of 55: £230 each)

357 SLEEPING £ 145
etching
Margaret Condon
(edition of 15: £100 each)

358 LAYERS OF MEMORY 1 £ 1,750
silver gelatin photo emulsion print and mixed media
Hiroto Hakamada

359 IN THE GARDEN £ 3,650
oil
Ishbel Myerscough

360 SHRINE FOR A DRIFTER £ 1,575
acrylic and gouache on paper
Joseph Schneider

361 GEOMETRIC TERRY £ 355
mixed media print
John Miles
(edition of 75: £300 each)

362 NIGHTSHIFT £ 120
drypoint, engraving
Martin Saull
(edition of 100: £95 each)

363 UNTITLED £ 120
screenprint
Matthew Green
(edition of 50: £60 each)

364 PINK SUMMER £ 380
pastel
Jeannette Hayes

365 ACTAEON AND DIANA £ 180
wood engraving
Jane Lydbury
(edition of 60: £140 each)

366 PORTUGUESE CART £ 140
copperplate engraving
Brian Hanscomb
(edition of 95: £100 each)

367 TIME AND TIDE £ 150
woodcut
Martin Saull
(edition of 100: £125 each)

368 ONE-TWO-THREE... £ 220
etching
Sandra Millar
(edition of 50: £180 each)

369 PJs 1 £ 300
linocut
Wayne Robinson
(edition of 50: £250 each)

370 SIX BOYS £ 495
etching
Jessie Brennan
(edition of 10: £395 each)

371 FEMALE NUDE, NO. 4 £ 295
digitial print
Edd Pearman
(edition of 30: £195 each)

372 30 ST. MARY AXE, GOING WEST £ 195
woodcut
Sasa Marinkov
(edition of 30: £145 each)

373 NASHNER LISSED BACK OF GRAAT BRITUN £ 335
copper plate etching
David Borrington
(edition of 42: £210 each)

374 A PRAM £ 140
wood engraving
Joseph Sloan
(edition of 65: £120 each)

375 THE THIRD POLICEMAN – FOX £ 110
etching and aquatint
Adam Wardle
(edition of 33: £80 each)

376 RACOON £ 150
soft-ground etching
Sylvia Eaves
(edition of 20: £105 each)

377 BURNING THE TREE £ 525
etching
Adrian Bartlett
(edition of 50: £450 each)

378 BLUE TIT £ 150
wood engraving print
Sarah Banfield
(edition of 10: £135 each)

379 WINCHES £ 150
etching and aquatint
Joseph Winkelman
(edition of 150: £100 each)

380 BLACK HOUSE £ 140
etching and aquatint
Sam Marshall
(edition of 65: £120 each)

381 PEBBLE WHALE £ 120
linocut
Andrew Carter
(edition of 50: £80 each)

382 MAKING SPACE FOR THE OLYMPICS 2012 £ 500
woodcut
Marianne Fox Ockinga
(edition of 50: £450 each)

383 SHEEP GRAZING WINTER LLWYNHIR £ 450
lithograph
Diana Armfield RA
(edition of 150: £400 each)

384 ESTUARY II £ 220
etching
Nicholas Grimshaw PRA
(edition of 20: £180 each)

385 BARN OWL £ 250
etching
Aileen Jampel
(edition of 25: £200 each)

386 SAUSAGE £ 145
lithograph
Robin Smart
(edition of 65: £110 each)

387 ME AS SEBALD £ 270
etching
Michael Hall
(edition of 21: £220 each)

388 SIREN #16 £ 350
linocut print on paper
Andrew Miller
(edition of 3: £300 each)

389 M. PARDUE £ 1,932
from a series of 15 framed pencil drawings on paper
Marie Harnett

390 SIREN #17 £ 350
linocut print on paper
Andrew Miller
(edition of 3: £300 each)

391 WINTER HARE £ 125
mezzotint
Debby Mason
(edition of 60: £95 each)

392 THE PENSIVE SELIMA RECLINED £ 215
etching and aquatint
Carl March
(edition of 75: £165 each)

393 COSSACK DANCERS £ 365
etching
Cordelia Cembrowicz
(edition of 20: £325 each)

394 BALANCING MAN £ 200
etching
Anthony Farrell
(edition of 50: £150 each)

395 LOWER LEA VALLEY IN SNOW £ 170
etching
Nicholas Middleton
(edition of 50: £130 each)

396 EDWARD £ 525
aquatint
Peter Freeth RA
(edition of 30: £450 each)

397 GIRL II £ 420
drypoint print
Anna Gardiner
(edition of 15: £320 each)

398 FIGURE APPROACHING THE BRITISH MUSEUM £ 472
soft-ground etching
Celia Paul
(edition of 15: £397 each)

399 LIBERTY OF LONDON £ 260
etching and aquatint
Samuel Hubbard
(edition of 40: £200 each)

400 VILLA SARACENO, ANDREA PALLADIO £ 475
pencil on paper
Richard Hutchinson
(edition of 25: £275 each)

401 AT SEA £ 265
etching
Matthew Ablitt
(edition of 50: £165 each)

402 COMPOUND CAPERS £ 340
etching
Michael Reid
(edition of 30: £280 each)

403 FLY ON THE WALL £ 165
etching
Paul Hawdon
(edition of 40: £135 each)

404 NIGHTCAP £ 235
aquatint etching
Frederic Morris
(edition of 18: £195 each)

405 GRASP £ 1,400
pencil on paper
Catherine Riley

406 ESTUARY I £ 220
etching
Nicholas Grimshaw PRA
(edition of 20: £180 each)

407 YOUNG UNICORN £ 240
etching and drypoint on paper
Mick Rooney RA
(edition of 100: £180 each)

408 SOMETHING DRIVES HIM TO IT... £ 210
etching
Peter Ford
(edition of 100: £170 each)

409 MAKING SPACE £ 175
etching
Anthony Dyson
(edition of 75: £130 each)

410 HAMBLEDON HILL £ 220
wood engraving
Howard Phipps
(edition of 150: £160 each)

411 APPARITION £ 985
silverpoint
Dylan Waldron

412 A WINTER IN THE HILLS £ 675
etching
David L Carpanini
(edition of 30: £490 each)

413 THORN TREE £ 165
aquatint etching
Carole De Jong
(edition of 25: £130 each)

414 WREN £ 179
drypoint and watercolour
Richard Spare
(edition of 100: £120 each)

415 FOUNDATIONS £ 230
calcography print on paper
Rocio Alcaman
(edition of 99: £200 each)

416 HONOUR £ 145
etching
Ellie Curtis
(edition of 50: £90 each)

417 NIGHT 1 £ 250
woodcut
Wayne Robinson
(edition of 30: £225 each)

418 J. M. W. TURNER ABOUT TO PUT CALM TO THE FACE £ 250
OF THE ONCOMING MAELSTROM
etching and aquatint
John Ross
(edition of 75: £200 each)

419 THE WESTERING MOON £ 250
etching and aquatint
David Parry
(edition of 100: £150 each)

420 OUT OF TIME £ 475
watercolour and gouache on paper
Lilo Fromm

421 CAT WALK £ 185
etching
Christopher Salmon
(edition of 100: £145 each)

422 FLEA £ 250
hard-ground copperplate etching
Lauren Drescher
(edition of 20: £180 each)

423 BUMBLE BEE £ 200
aquatint and etching
Diana Howorth
(edition of 10: £175 each)

424 DOORWAY £ 1,932
from a series of 15 framed pencil drawings on paper
Marie Harnett

425 FISHING BOAT £ 120
linocut
Andrew Carter
(edition of 50: £80 each)

426 NIGHT GAME £ 245
etching
John Duffin
(edition of 90: £195 each)

427 GROVE HILL £ 320
etching
Bella Easton
(edition of 50: £280 each)

428 MYTH £ 150
wood engraving
Anna Alcock
(edition of 20: £115 each)

429 DEFIANCE £ 90
chine collé and wood engraving
Anna Alcock
(edition of 20: £75 each)

430 HEADLAND ST. DAVIDS £ 270
etching
Austin Cole
(edition of 55: £230 each)

431 NEW YORKER £ 130
etching
Alan Smith
(edition of 90: £100 each)

432 HOME BEFORE THE DARKNESS FALLS £ 160
etching
Anthony Salter
(edition of 150: £120 each)

433 URBAN SPACE 1 £ 500
pastel on paper
Oona Hassim

434 IF I PROMISE TO STOP SENDING YOU POEMS, £ 320
MAY I HAVE MY PEN BACK?
ink and oil on board
Richard Dinnis

435 EIRA'S SHOES £ 150
silkscreen print
Lesley O'Reilly
(edition of 25: £100 each)

436 NIGHT TIME IN BAT SHLOMO £ 175
etching, hardground and drypoint
Naomi Alexander
(edition of 25: £120 each)

437 MAKE SOME ROOM £ 650
oil on board
Emily Marbach

438 PORTRAIT OF A GIRL SITTING IN A CHAIR £ 12,000
bronze relief
James Butler RA
(edition of 4: £12,000 each)

439 REFLECTIONS £ 1,150
pen, ink and crayons
John Farman

440 WALKERS ON BOYARDVILLE BEACH £ 495
mixed media, acrylic on paper
Tony Scrivener

441 JANUARY KING £ 1,200
oil
Stephen Rose

442 UNFINISHED TRI PLANE £ 2,500
oil
Liam Thompson

443 ERIC'S CAFE £ 5,000
oil
John Peace

444 NINE £ 1,500
oil
Martin Leman

445 DOORWAY, DARK THEATRE £ 995
oil on board
Jean Palmer

446 WEST BAY £ 800
oil
David Payne

447 THE TURQUOISE NECKLACE £ 950
oil
Chrissie Birchall

448 NEWCASTLE NIGHT £ 70
oil
Susan Abel

449 SILENT ALL THESE YEARS £ 600
mixed media
Julie Lush

450 SMALL TOWN £ 1,800
egg tempera and oil on panel
Michael Johnson

451 ALBA £ 12,000
oil on canvas over board
Nicolas Granger-Taylor

452 BLACK AND CITRUS £ 800
oil
Christine Hipkiss

453	**RED PIANO** *mixed* Rosa Sepple	£ 950
454	**STILL LIFE** *watercolour* Richard Selby	£ 800
455	**MARLENE** *acrylic* Jennifer Harris	£ 575
456	**WATER GLASS** *oil* Ann Heat	£ 850
457	**THE LAST SPROUTS** *oil on board* Jocelyn Wickham	£ 900
458	**A FEW CHERRIES** *oil on board* Barbara Richardson	£ 780
459	**MAKING SPACE** *glazed fired tile* Bernard Rebuck	£ 300
460	**LAST POSTE** *digital printed tile, collage* Bernard Rebuck	£ 250
461	**CAMPANULA** *oil on board* Jocelyn Clarke	£ 540
462	**FLOATING FLIPPERS** *oil* David Madden	£ 900
463	**PIGEON AND WADER** *oil* Peter Perry	£ 700

464 WONKY'S NICHE IN MY MEMORY £ 1,350
oil
Anne Songhurst

**465 THE WHITE SOCK
(LEONARD AND ROXANNE ROSOMAN)** £ 6,000
oil on paper
Eileen Hogan

466 WOOLWORTHS £ 1,375
oil
Simon Turvey

467 SPECIMEN JARDIN £ 3,250
oil
Nicholas Pace

468 A SPECIAL FLOWER £ 450
acrylic
Jill Leman

469 FLOWERS IN JUNE IN THE MOUSTIER JUG £ 6,500
oil
Diana Armfield RA

470 BELLAGIO, A ROOM WITH A VIEW £ 1,100
oil
Peter R Hunt

471 PAUL SMITH II £ 1,350
oil on board
Oscar Whicheloe

472 THE BEGUILING VIEW, VENICE £ 2,500
pastel
Diana Armfield RA

473 MAHÉ, SEYCHELLES £ 990
acrylic
Angela Braven

474 U-BAHN, ALEXANDERPLATZ £ 1,000
white chalk on blackboard
Emma Stibbon

475 SHE SAID TO ME £ 1,700
iron oxides, marble dust, acrylic gel
David Brayne

476 VILLAGE GARDEN £ 1,750
oil
Louis Turpin

477 LITTLE KINGDOM £ 4,400
acrylic
Cedric Huson

478 MORNING COFFEE £ 595
acrylic on paper, canvas
Tony Scrivener

479 RAMSGATE HARBOUR, LATE SUMMER £ 650
oil
Margot Bandola

480 A JOURNEY THROUGH TIME, LIGHT AND SPACE IN WALES £ 1,150
oil
Maurice Sheppard

481 FEEDING THE HENS, BELOW SAN GIMIGNANO £ 7,000
oil
Diana Armfield RA

482 SAVILLE ROW II £ 1,350
oil on board
Oscar Whicheloe

483 WAITING £ 1,500
oil on board
Liam O'Farrell

484 ADMIRING THE BABIES, VENICE £ 5,000
oil
Diana Armfield RA

485 OBJECTS £ 1,100
oil
David Warrillow

486 A 470, PURPLE SKY £ 2,500
oil on board
Danny Markey

487 DUTCH POTS II £ 2,250
oil
David Stubbs

488 SEA SEEN £ 1,200
oil and wax on board
Savva Savva

489 PANSIES £ 1,700
oil
Ian Parker

490 LAST OF ENGLAND £ 695
oil
A Lincoln Taber

491 SOLACE £ 850
gouache on ply board
Mick Owens

492 LOOKING AHEAD (2) £ 2,500
oil on canvas on board
Pedro Baztan Rodriguez

493 UNTITLED (HOLED) £ 325
oil
Mark Evans

494 STUDY 1 £ 350
oil on MDF
Hannah Birkett

495 HOT RIVALRY UNDER THE EQUATORIAL PASSIONATE £ 3,400
SUN, VANUATU
monoprint
Michael B White

496 PINK CYCLAMEN £ 495
watercolour
Rosemary Farrer

497 DAFFODIL £ 950
oil
Michael Whittlesea

498 THE BEACH EXPRESS £ 500
oil
Dariel Raven

499 BEACH HOUSES £ 500
oil
Muriel Mallows

500 STILL KNIFE £ 2,900
acrylic
Tim Gustard

501 THAMESVIEW WITH THE OBELISK NEAR £ 3,250
TEDDINGTON LOCK
oil
Patricia Buckley

502 PALMYRA £ 550
oil on board
Richard Rees

503 DISCUSSING BERYL'S BYPASS £ 700
acrylic
David Fawcett

504 COAST £ 1,500
oil
Martin Leman

505 FLOWER PAINTING £ 5,200
oil and alkyd on wood panel
Simon Monk

506 A BAD INDULGENCE £ 150
photo print
Claire Davidge

507 SWANSONG FOR A COZY COUPE £ 1,500
acrylic
Martin Grover

508 ANY SPACE FOR A BISCUIT? £ 300
oil
Amanda Coleman

509 ANY SPACE FOR CAKE? £ 300
oil
Amanda Coleman

510 WHITE LIGHT £ 995
oil
Ingrid Wilkins

511 KATHERINE £ 1,850
oil on linen
June Redfern

512 EVENING £ 2,650
oil on linen
June Redfern

513 MAGNIFICENT SUE, 2006 £ 750
oil on paper
Vladimir Karnachev

514 MASTER CLASS £ 250
oil
Jane Stallwood

515 THE LAST LEMONS £ 1,250
acrylic on board
David Humphreys

516 BLACKFRIARS END £ 350
acrylic
Lee Madgwick

517 UNKISSED £ 700
abrasive drawing
Alison Rylands

518 ORCHID ON PINK T SHIRT £ 500
oil on panel
Margaret Foreman

519 THE ACCOUNTANTS OFFICE
thread
Ann Ward

£ 550

520 SHEEP SHELTERING, WINTER AT LLWYNHIR
lithograph
Diana Armfield RA
(edition of 150: £400 each)

£ 450

521 PINK NUCLEAR CAT
acrylic
Ron Sims

£ 550

522 TUNNEL
oil on board
David Woodall

£ 250

523 SUNLIGHT AND A WOMAN READING
oil
Peter Kelly

£ 4,000

524 CORSICAN DAWN
oil
Antoine Robin

£ 450

525 LAST TUBE
oil
John Duffin

£ 2,750

526 COFFEE GRINDER
oil
James Crittenden

£ 1,800

527 TRIPLE REFLECTION
oil
Christopher Glanville

£ 675

528 LIBITUM I
oil
Toni McGreachan

£ 685

529 THE PAINTER
watercolour pigment, acrylic gel
David Brayne

£ 1,700

530 MARKING TIME *acrylic* Kate Talbot		£ 300
531 FISHFULL THINKING *coloured inks* Leonard Manasseh RA		£ 321
532 NUDE, LYING BACK I *chalk* Bernard Dunstan RA		£ 975
533 THE DEALER *old books and beeswax* Ann Winder-Boyle		£ 750
534 WHITE SAILS *oil* Francis Tinsley		£ 800
535 DOOR INTO THE KITCHEN *oil* Bernard Dunstan RA		£ 7,500
536 WILHELMINA MMIX *pencil and charcoal on paper* Warren Baldwin		£ 1,600
537 EXOTIC PLANT *acrylic* Jill Leman		£ 485
538 TIME UNCHANGED *paper, college, ink, watercolour* Jo Fox		£ 1,500
539 ANEMONES IN DECO VASE *gouache* Anne Goldberg		£ 1,200
540 CAROUSEL CHAIRS, STRASBOURG *watercolour and body colour* Pamela Crewe		£ 450

541 FRIGILIANA £1,250
oil
Joan Elliott Bates

542 WINTER WINDOW £850
acrylic and mixed media
Gail Murray

543 SUNBEDS AND SWIMMERS £1,100
oil
Lucy Pratt

544 DRESSING, DARK MORNING £7,500
oil
Bernard Dunstan RA

545 LOOKING AHEAD (1) £2,500
oil on canvas on board
Pedro Baztan Rodriguez

546 CAFÉ AU NATUREL £1,750
egg tempera and oils
Marcelle Milo-Gray

547 SUNDAY MORNING £1,400
oil on board
Marion Pritchard

548 NUDE LYING BACK II £975
chalk
Bernard Dunstan RA

549 UNDER THE MOON £380
acrylic
Alison Nicholson

550 WASTE TRAIN £490
oil and acrylic on board
Andrew Pearson

551 REFLECTED STATES, BRICKING IN £200
inkjet and watercolour on card
Amy Thomas
(edition of 100: £75 each)

552 MOSTLY RED £ 500
acrylic
Georgina Rowbottom

553 MEETING BY MOONLIGHT £ 1,300
acrylic
Ian Bliss

554 BLUE INTERIOR £ 4,000
acrylic
Cedric Huson

555 STAMPEDE £ 550
charcoal, chalk and coloured pencil
William Wright

556 SUMMERTIME £ 500
oil
Dariel Raven

557 THE BARBER AND THE BOOKIE £ 1,500
oil
Charles Debenham

558 PLAYING WITH FORMS OF 'J' £ 600
drawing
Rania Bellou

559 PLAYING WITH FORMS OF 'I' £ 600
drawing
Olrania Bellouq

560 FREEHOLDER £ 200
etching with handcolouring in watercolour and oil paint
Tisna Westerhof
(edition of 24: £180 each)

561 DREAM PAINTING, 13.6.2008, PERFORMER FALLING £ 500
oil on board
Jane Gifford

562 THROUGH THE WINDOW £ 690
oil
Sandrine Rey

563 BALANCING ELEPHANT £ 4,000
bronze
Jim Unsworth
(edition of 12: £4,000 each)

564 DANCER HOLDING HER SHOES, 2009 £ 8,500
bronze
James Butler RA
(edition of 10: £8,500 each)

565 ISAMBARD KINGDOM BRUNEL SKETCH FOR £ 10,500
A PORTRAIT STATUE
bronze
James Butler RA
(edition of 8: £10,500 each)

566 DANCER IN A FLOWERED DRESS £ 8,000
bronze
James Butler RA
(edition of 10: £8,000 each)

567	**BANDERSNATCH 2008** *coloured pencil on paper* Michael Kidner RA	£ 25,000
568	**LAPIS** *oil* Humphrey Ocean RA	£ 15,000
569	**WHITE** *oil* Humphrey Ocean RA	£ 15,000
570	**VERMILION** *oil* Humphrey Ocean RA	£ 15,000
571	**AZURE** *oil* Humphrey Ocean RA	£ 15,000
572	**ORANGE** *oil* Humphrey Ocean RA	£ 15,000
573	**GREEN** *oil* Humphrey Ocean RA	£ 15,000
574	**THE ROSE (III)** *acrylic on plywood* Cy Twombly Hon RA	NFS
575	**UNTITLED 2002** *oil* Richard Smith	£ 60,000

576 H.2.N.Y DYING PIANO PLAYS ITS LAST NOTE, 2007 £ 12,000
oil stick on paper
Michael Landy RA

577 DRAWING (3), 2007 £ 18,000
charcoal on paper
Michael Landy RA

578 INSIDE OUTSIDE £ 7,500
acrylic on linen
C Morey de Morand

579 17, I WANT IT BACK, THAT FEELING AGAIN £ 90,000
oil
Tracey Emin RA

580 A TIDAL PORT-HOLE NFS
oil on board
Jeffery Camp RA

581 POPPY £ 4,500
oil on board
Jeffery Camp RA

582 STORM £ 15,000
oil
Jeffery Camp RA

583 BEACHY HEAD £ 5,000
oil on board
Jeffery Camp RA

584 BIG BEN £ 5,500
oil on board
Jeffery Camp RA

585 ALICE & DOROTHY £ 8,000
oil on canvas on board
Jeffery Camp RA

586 WATCHING FIREFLIES BY THE LAKE £ 15,000
acrylic
Maurice Cockrill RA

587 OLD DEMONS PLAYING   £ 15,000
acrylic
Maurice Cockrill RA

588 NIGHT MUSIC   £ 15,000
acrylic
Maurice Cockrill RA

589 DREAM POOL   £ 15,000
acrylic
Maurice Cockrill RA

590 EVERYMAN 2009   £ 8,000
oil
Stephen Chambers RA

591 LILLIES (WITH BEADS) 2009   £ 8,000
oil
Stephen Chambers RA

592 ARACURIA 2009   £ 8,000
oil
Stephen Chambers RA

593 BATHROOM / BLACK MIRROR/FOX 2009   £ 24,000
oil
Stephen Chambers RA

594 PORTRAIT OF CAREL WEIGHT NUMBER 2   £ 30,000
pencil, pastel and gold leaf on paper
Leonard McComb RA

595 PORTRAIT OF REBECCA   £ 30,000
pencil, ink, and pastel on paper
Leonard McComb RA

596 ZARRIN SLEEPING   £ 40,000
watercolour on RWS paper mounted on cotton
Leonard McComb RA

597 MAJORELLE 4   £ 9,200
acrylic on paper
Gillian Ayres RA

598 MAJORELLE 3 £ 9,200
acrylic on paper
Gillian Ayres RA

599 THE SUN SHONE FROM A DIFFERENT PLACE £ 46,000
oil
Gillian Ayres RA

600 EULOGY £ 15,000
acrylic
Gus Cummins RA

601 OPPOSITION £ 15,000
oil
Gus Cummins RA

602 STUDY FOR GOLDEN HANDSHAKE NO. 3 £ 700
acrylic on board
Stephen Farthing RA

603 STUDY FOR GOLDEN HANDSHAKE NO. 1 £ 700
acrylic on board
Stephen Farthing RA

604 STUDY FOR GOLDEN HANDSHAKE NO. 2 £ 700
acrylic on board
Stephen Farthing RA

605 NO. 32, FROM A SERIES 'GHIRLANDA', 2006–07 £ 6,500
acrylic
Jennifer Durrant RA

606 NO. 18, FROM A SERIES 'GHIRLANDA', 2007 £ 6,500
acrylic on canvas on board
Jennifer Durrant RA

607 NO. 22, FROM A SERIES 'GHIRLANDA', 2007 £ 6,500
acrylic on canvas on board
Jennifer Durrant RA

608 AWAKE, FROM A SERIES 'GHIRLANDA', 2006–09 £ 40,000
acrylic
Jennifer Durrant RA

609	**BRILLIG 2009**	£ 6,000
	coloured pencil on paper	
	Michael Kidner RA	

610	**FRUMIOUS 2009**	£ 6,000
	coloured pencil on paper	
	Michael Kidner RA	

611	**REEF 2008**	£ 6,000
	coloured pencil on paper	
	Michael Kidner RA	

612	**SIMCA 2009**	£ 6,000
	coloured pencil on paper	
	Michael Kidner RA	

613	**VERTIGO II 2008 – 2009**	£ 9,500
	acrylic and collage on canvas	
	Anthony Whishaw RA	

614	**MALE AND FEMALE NUDE WEARING MASKS (TONY AND MAGGIE)**	NFS
	oil on canvas on mdf	
	Marcus Harvey	

615	**SEASCAPE WITH APPROACHING RAIN CLOUDS 2007 – 2009**	£ 20,000
	acrylic and collage on canvas	
	Anthony Whishaw RA	

616	**DOWNSTREAM THAW 2007 – 2009**	£ 12,000
	acrylic and collage on canvas	
	Anthony Whishaw RA	

617	**BLUEINTENT**	£ 12,000
	acrylic	
	Frank Bowling RA	

618	**RIPERED**	£ 12,000
	acrylic	
	Frank Bowling RA	

619	**SOUNDSYELLOW**	£ 12,000
	acrylic	
	Frank Bowling RA	

620	**TRAVELLER**	£ 12,000
	acrylic	
	Frank Bowling RA	

621	**CHINESECHANCE**	£ 12,000
	acrylic	
	Frank Bowling RA	

622	**LAMPTHRUST**	£ 12,000
	acrylic	
	Frank Bowling RA	

623	**11 MISTY LANDSCAPES**	£ 26,910
	oil	
	Lisa Milroy RA	

624	**SUMMER BREEZE**	£ 17,940
	oil	
	Lisa Milroy RA	

625	**APT NO.2**	£ 5,946
	hand painting in acrylic on paper with carborundum printing	
	Gillian Ayres RA	

626	**CONJUNCTION SANGIOVESE, ARCO**	£ 51,750
	oil on canvas on wood	
	Joe Tilson RA	

627	**FLOWERS OF GOLD**	£ 13,000
	oil	
	Philip Sutton RA	

628	**BREEZE OF THE MORNING!**	£ 8,300
	oil	
	Philip Sutton RA	

629	**THE WIZARD OF PEMBROKESHIRE**	£ 7,500
	oil	
	Philip Sutton RA	

630	**FLOWERS FOR IVAN TURGENEV**	£ 7,500
	oil	
	Philip Sutton RA	

631 THE MAGIC SEA £ 8,250
oil
Philip Sutton RA

632 BLUE SWELL £ 18,000
foam pvc and steel and wood
Phillip King PPRA

633 YELLOW BEAM £ 6,500
steel and plastic
Phillip King PPRA

634 BASTIDE £ 5,500
mixed media
Phillip King PPRA

635 BLUE SLICER £ 5,000
plastic pvc
Phillip King PPRA

636 YELLOW LEAN £ 5,000
plastic pvc
Phillip King PPRA

637 UNTITLED (DESIRE) *
acrylic on aluminium
Michael Craig-Martin RA

638 ANGER £ 4,964
from a series of seven screenprints
Michael Craig-Martin RA
(edition of 30: £3,738 each)

639 DANTE I, 2009 £ 23,000
acrylic
Albert Irvin RA

640 DANTE III, 2009 £ 8,050
acrylic
Albert Irvin RA

641 LIMEHOUSE II, 2008 £ 8,050
acrylic
Albert Irvin RA

* Refer to Sales Desk

642 CONJUNCTION HESIOD, KYTINOS £ 40,250
oil on canvas on wood
Joe Tilson RA

643 SMAK: MAK (A MUSE UM) £ 22,425
digital neon and associated electrical components
mounted on aluminium panel
Ben Langlands & Nikki Bell
(edition of 3)

644 FINESTRA VENEZIANA SAN ZANIPOLO £ 17,250
acrylic, glass, lattimo glass on wood relief
Joe Tilson RA

645 18 HOLES £ 2,500
inkjet, pencil and pen on paper
Richard Wilson RA

646 FUTURIST MANIFESTO (DIPPED) £ 1,400
hardback book and gloss paint
Shane Bradford

647 JOINT'S JUMPING £ 5,000
photograph, wire, print on paper
Richard Wilson RA

648 MEDUSA £ 6,000
stainless steel powdered coated and brass
Bryan Kneale RA

649 MIND OUT OF TIME, 2009 *
fingerprints on driftwood
Richard Long RA

650 DRIFTER £ 1,500
fired-glazed clay
Annie Turner

651 SILENT LIGHT – 2 £ 3,200
stainless steel
Ann Christopher RA
(edition of 9: £3,200 each)

652 S# 2 NFS
light jet print mounted on dibond panel
Beate Gutschow

653 S # 25 £ 15,200
light jet print mounted on dibond panel
Beate Gutschow

* Refer to Sales Desk

654 WHITE LIGHT £ 2,900
sterling silver
Ann Christopher RA
(edition of 9: £2,900 each)

655 CUTS UP CUTS DOWN, 2009 £ 14,000
limewood
David Nash RA

656 BULLET DRAWING £ 5,875
lead bullet drawn into wire
Cornelia Parker

657 FOUR IDENTICAL SHAPES £ 2,950
brass
John Carter RA
(edition of 3: £2,950 each)

658 ASSEMBLY GOUACHE (REF: G-2008-10) £ 8,650
gouache and pencil on paper
Ian McKeever RA

659 ASSEMBLY GOUACHE (REF: G-2008-13) £ 7,025
gouache and pencil on paper
Ian McKeever RA

660 ASSEMBLY GOUACHE (REF: G-2008-9) £ 8,650
gouache and pencil on paper
Ian McKeever RA

661 QUANTUM VOID VI, 2009 £ 230,000
6mm square section mild steel bar
Antony Gormley RA

662 TREE LINE £ 12,000
mixed media
Mick Moon RA

663 INFORMER V *
bronze, paint and gold leaf
Bill Woodrow RA

664 SPASM £ 1,750
pen and ink drawing on paper
Wendy Smith

Refer to Sales Desk

665	**SHUDDER**	£ 1,750
	pen and ink drawing on paper	
	Wendy Smith	

666	**CROSSING**	£ 12,000
	ink on japanese paper, bronze	
	Alison Wilding RA	

667	**TUNDRA 3**	£ 3,163
	oil paint, ink and coloured pencil	
	Bill Woodrow RA	

668	**TUNDRA 1**	£ 3,163
	oil paint, ink and coloured pencil	
	Bill Woodrow RA	

669	**TUNDRA 2**	£ 3,163
	oil paint, ink and coloured pencil	
	Bill Woodrow RA	

670	**TUNDRA 4**	£ 3,163
	oil paint, ink, coloured pencil	
	Bill Woodrow RA	

671	**CENTERFOLD**	*
	bronze and gold leaf	
	Bill Woodrow RA	
	(edition of 8)	

672	**SMALL STUDY FOR MONKEY PUZZLE II**	NFS
	gouache on fibre-based photograph	
	Tacita Dean	

673	**NO GLOVE, NO LOVE**	£ 3,866
	bronze	
	Peter Oloya	
	(edition of 9: £3,866 each)	

674	**THE SPACE BETWEEN – 1**	£ 780
	hand-cut etching	
	Ann Christopher RA	
	(edition of 20: £700 each)	

* Refer to Sales Desk

675	**THE SPACE BETWEEN – 2**	£ 780
	hand-cut etching	
	Ann Christopher RA	
	(edition of 20: £700 each)	

676	**THE SPACE BETWEEN – 3**	£ 780
	hand-cut etching	
	Ann Christopher RA	
	(edition of 20: £700 each)	

677	**LIKE THUNDER**	£ 48,300
	polished wood	
	Nigel Hall RA	

678	**DARK FALL**	£ 3,750
	mixed media	
	Kenneth Draper RA	

679	**PERFORMANCE**	£ 1,250
	carbon fibre, lead	
	Timothy Sandys	
	(edition of 8: £1,250 each)	

680	**TRANSMISSION. F**	£ 4,800
	newspapers	
	Yoshimi Kihara	

681	**GEMINI**	£ 20,000
	mirror polished stainless steel	
	Bryan Kneale RA	

682	**OVER HERE**	£ 2,500
	cherry wood	
	John Cobb	

683	**GALATEA**	£ 2,900
	carved bronze	
	Bryan Kneale RA	

684	**ATLAS**	£ 3,750
	bronze	
	Bryan Kneale RA	

685 BERE ISLAND BOWL, 2009 £ 25,000
composite materials (unique)
Eilis O'Connell

686 POLYMORPH £ 5,385
bronze
Jon Buck
(edition of 10: £5,385 each)

687 HIGH WIRE £ 69,000
painted aluminium
Allen Jones RA

688 CORALLIUM RUBRUM II, 2008 £ 22,000
clear cast resin and coral
Eilis O'Connell

689 GLORIA MUNDI NFS
bronze
Marcus Harvey

| 690 | **GLADSTONE**
mixed media on triplewall
Danny Rolph | £ 8,000 |

| 691 | **CANNONBALL TREE, SEYCHELLES**
acrylic
Angela Braven | £ 6,000 |

| 692 | **MAKING SPACE**
oil
Irene Spee | £ 2,700 |

| 693 | **ARMS UP**
oil
Roy Oxlade | £ 16,000 |

| 694 | **UNITITLED II**
lasercut print
Jenny Smith
(edition of 15: £300 each) | £ 350 |

| 695 | **LADY BEE HYDRANGEA**
oil on panel
Melanie Miller | £ 1,600 |

| 696 | **ROCK**
oil
Amanda Ansell | £ 800 |

| 697 | **COASTLINE**
oil, acrylic, clay, emulsion, charcoal on cardboard
Vassilis Pafilis | £ 1,300 |

| 698 | **AT THE EDGE, CLIFFS AT ST. MARGARET'S, LOOKING NORTH**
oil
George Rowlett | £ 7,200 |

699 HERE AND NOW £ 4,000
oil
Ian Humphreys

700 A MAN AND A WOMAN £ 9,000
oil
Rose Wylie

701 NIGHT RIDERS £ 1,700
acrylic
Matt Mounsey

702 ESTUARY £ 2,000
watercolour and collage
Philip Reeves

703 UNDO DO 2008 £ 1,600
mixed media on paper on board
Gordon Faulds

704 THE ILLUSION OF OTHERNESS £ 1,000
mixed media
Hana Horack-Elyafi

705 SOUND OF YELLOW ANGELS, 2008 £ 6,000
acrylic
Bill Henderson

706 UNTITLED £ 2,900
encaustic on canvas over panel
Grant Watson

707 HONG KONG PAINTING £ 2,900
oil and wax on canvas
Grant Watson

708 AKHENATEN'S LITTLE GROUPIE SO BREATHLESS £ 4,000
IN CHINCHILLA (RED)
mixed media
Mary Malenoir

709 TROJANS £ 6,000
oil
Arthur Neal

710 CLADOPHORA WORSHIP £ 6,000
stucco lucido fresco on panel
Carey Mortimer

711 SLIPROAD £ 2,000
oil and acrylic
Deborah Burnstone

712 DISRUPTION I £ 3,500
mixed media on canvas
Nandita Chaudhuri

713 MAKING SPACE: APPARTAMENTI VENDITA, VENICE £ 2,500
tempera and oil on linen on board
Peter Beeson

714 TIGHTLY PACKED £ 5,700
acrylic
Novette Cummings

715 CART I £ 450
acrylic
Ian David Baker

716 PINK DRESSES AND PONY PLAITS £ 795
pencil and ink on wallpaper
Kerry Phippen

717 MAY F IRELAND 2008 £ 3,500
watercolour
Trevor Sutton

718 ARCANE SEEK (MOON CANOPY) £ 4,000
acrylic and latex on linen
Hannah Maybank

719 SMALL BLACK BOX JAN '09 £ 950
oil
Jane Lewis

720 MANGO, STUDIO £ 2,500
oil
Sarah Armstrong-Jones

721 EXTERIOR SPACE, KYOTO £ 600
acrylic and paper collage
Sylvia Paul

722 BRECON BEACON £ 3,800
oil on linen
David Hegarty

723 YELLOW £ 3,250
oil
Arthur Neal

724 A RETURN TO EMOTION, MARCH 2009 £ 2,000
acrylic
Geoffrey Clarke RA

725 REFLECTION £ 380
mixed media
Christine Heider

726 NOMAD £ 800
mixed media on canvas
Iskender Nurdan

727 THREE TUNNELS £ 400
oil
Jeni Johnson

728 PENELOPE £ 650
oil on unpicked and re-sewn canvas
Bridget H Jackson

729 ESCAPE FROM UNIFORMITY £ 2,000
linen cloth, paper clay, arylic and oil paint
Noriko Watanabe

730 METAMORPHOSIS FROM STILL LIFE WITH £ 19,000
BLUE CLOTH II, 2005
oil on linen
Gary Wragg

731 A RETURN TO EMOTION, APRIL 2009 £ 3,000
acrylic
Geoffrey Clarke RA

732 CROSSING CURRENTS £ 12,000
plywood, linen, oil paint
Arthur Wilson

733 DISRUPTION II £ 3,500
mixed media on canvas
Nandita Chaudhuri

734 DANCING IN THE DARK £ 7,600
oil paint on linen
David Royle

735 MENTAL SPACE £ 2,500
acrylic
Luciana Meazza

736 NO. 25, FROM A SERIES 'GHIRLANDA', 2007 £ 8,000
acrylic
Jennifer Durrant RA

737 NO. 24, FROM A SERIES 'GHIRLANDA', 2007 £ 8,000
acrylic on canvas on board
Jennifer Durrant RA

738 THAMESSCAPE 1 £ 1,000
mixed media
Bridget Boulting

739 WEDDING DRESS £ 4,400
collagraph, paper and canvas
Julia Hamilton

740 ARTICULATING THE SPACES: STUDY £ 2,000
pencil, chalk, and gouache
Paul Newland

741 SNAPSHOTS 1 – STONEHENGE RIVERSIDE PROJECT £ 1,500
watercolour and pencil
Julia Midgley

742 THE BACK STEPS £ 7,600
oil on linen
David Royle

743 UNTITLED NO. 901 £ 660
faber castell on bfk rives
Helga Schmidt

744 SMALL PAINTING 3, 2008 £ 790
acrylic paint on birch-faced plywood
Nigel O'Neill

745 BROKEN SYMMETRY #2 £ 2,800
acrylic
Julie Umerle

746 TOO BIG- OR NOT TOO BIG? £ 1,950
black pen on white paper
Irene Lees

747 UNTITLED (POLICE SADDLE) Editions are available for sale
pencil on mylar (print: ink on mylar)
Patrick Gilmartin
(edition of 50: £500 each)

748 COLLAR II £ 5,200
steel, bioresin, fabric and gesso
Julie Major

749 CONVERTING £ 2,500
oil
Adrienne Blake

750 BLUE DRIFT £ 4,500
oil
Matthew Kolakowski

751 CLEARING GRANNIES ATTIC £ 2,500
oil
Adrienne Blake

752 KNOTTED CURTAIN AND BATH £ 8,000
oil
Roy Oxlade

753 SHEIKH ZAYED ROAD, DUBAI £ 10,750
conté crayon
Jeanette Barnes

754 I WISH MY GARDEN WAS REALLY LIKE THIS £ 7,500
acrylic
William Alsop RA

755 SANTON II £ 4,800
oil on canvas on board
Peter Clossick

756 MODEL CITIZEN, 2008 £ 30,000
acrylic
Derek Boshier

757 THE SPIRIT OF THE BEEHIVE, DAROCA, SPAIN £ 1,400
charcoal conté
Michael Davis

758 SHOT IN THE ARM COWBOY, 2007 £ 30,000
acrylic
Derek Boshier

759 COMPOSITION £ 675
oil
Janine Baldwin

760 POST INERT PHASE II CUBE B, 1968 £ 14,000
cast aluminium
Geoffrey Clarke RA

761 POST INERT PHASE II CUBE A, 1968 £ 14,000
cast aluminium
Geoffrey Clarke RA

762 POST INERT PHASE II PYRAMID, 1968 £ 17,500
cast aluminium
Geoffrey Clarke RA

763 ON TOP £ 1,700
papier mâché
Chris Dunseath

764 CONNECTIONS £ 900
steel and cement
Jaana Fowler

765 SINKER £ 1,800
fired-glazed clay
Annie Turner

766 DEEP RED LINE £ 4,800
italian statuary alabaster, resin and pigment
Jay Battle

767 IT'S FULL OF STARS £ 1,500
paper mâché
Chris Dunseath

768 STAIR DESIGN WORKING MODEL, FINAL STATE,   NFS
PRIVATE RESIDENCE, MODEL USED ON SITE FOR REFERENCE
mixed media
Eric Parry RA

769 JUICE BAR, MANCHESTER   £ 400
mesh
William Alsop RA

770 RESIDENTIAL TOWER, TORONTO   £ 750
acrylic
William Alsop RA

771 MEASURING PERSONAL SPACE   £ 4,800
bronze
Bill Scott

772 WEIGHTLESS SPACE FRAME   NFS
wood
Anon, SABE, University of Westminster

773 SWORDS METRO QUARTER   NFS
timber, acrylic and metal
Metropolitan Workshop

774 TIMBER ROOF SHELL   NFS
wood
Anon, SABE, University of Westminster

775 INVISIBLE UNIVERSITY, L.A.W.U.N. PROJECT #21.   £ 220
A WELL-SERVICED PRIMITIVE WEARS ELECTRO-SOCIAL
CAMOUFLAGE. GENERAL CONDITION: INCIDENTAL
PASTURALISM. TEST SITE ONE: CYBUCOLIA
digital print
Sara Shafiei
(edition of 25: £220 each)

776	**STUDY FOR IMPINGEMENT DRAWING: 2 ROOMS WITH BARLEY SUGAR TWIST** *acrylic, ink and aluminium* Gary Woodley	£ 2,400
777	**COLOURSPACE** *mixed media in perspex* Donald Smith	£ 5,000
778	**LIBRARY TOWER AND ARCHIVE IN THE RIVER THAMES** *ink on paper* Esther Rivas Adrover	£ 2,300
779	**SWEET SPOT II** *plaster polymer, fabric* Julie Major	£ 4,800
780	**L'EX MONASTERO** *bronze* Lidia Palumbi	NFS
781	**SHELTER 2** *bronze* Marian Fountain (edition of 40: £250 each)	£ 250
782	**SEED GROWTH** *cast iron and gold leaf* Dilys Jackson	£ 900
783	**SPACE MAKER** *kaolin paste and watercolour* Bernhard Stoezen	£ 1,200
784	**CHIRP CHIRP SOLDIERS** *fiberglass reinforced plastics* Suguru Takada	£ 2,200
785	**I-HUB CONCEPT SKETCH 3** *pencil* Paul Koralek RA	£ 225
786	**PULITZER FOUNDATION FOR THE ARTS, ST. LOUIS, 2001** *photographs* Tadao Ando Hon RA	NFS

787 BUTTERFLY CAN (MOTORISED) 2009 £ 2,800
mixed media construction
Tim Lewis

788 MEDAL MEDDLING WITH THE INSIDE £ 380
bronze
Jacqueline Stieger

789 UNTITLED NFS
acrylic and ink on paper box, cardboard and wood
Onofrio Chillemi

790 LONG VIEWS OF PARADISE £ 1,500
(DRAFTED BY: SARA SHAFIEI)
paper
White Table

791 CIVIL WAR RELIC £ 2,500
bronze
John Campion
(edition of 6: £2,500 each)

792 OCAD WITH TEDDY NFS
mixed media
William Alsop RA

793 GLASS WALL STUDY, 2009 NFS
perspex
Aurimas Bauzys

794 THE WINK, DEMOUNTABLE EVENTS PAVILION NFS
card, tights and sewing thread
Feix&Merlin Architects

795 CONCEPT MODEL FOR NEWPORT STATION, WALES NFS
model
Sir Nicholas Grimshaw PRA

796 PAPER WALL STUDIES, 2008 NFS
paper
Khadija Durbar

797 URBAN TRIPTYCH. HOUSING PROJECT FOR RIJEKA, £ 2,500
CROATIA
model
architektur.bn / Sasa Bradic, Ines Nizic

798 PALACE OF LABOUR (TURIN) MORPHOLOGY OF LIGHT AND STRUCTURE NFS
laser-printed model
Selvei Al-Assadi

799 SAVILL GARDENS VISITOR CENTRE NFS
model and hand-coloured drawings
Birds Portchmouth Russum Architects

800 PROJECT 373 NFS
architectural model
Marks Barfield Architects

801 CASTLE PARK CORNER, BRISTOL (MODEL BY: A MODELS) NFS
model
Sanei Hopkins Architects

802 RESPONSIVE MAGNETIC FAÇADE STUDY NFS
perspex and mdf
Anon, SABE, University of Westminster

803 MODEL FOR BAROMI HOUSE, LONDON NW8 (DESIGNED BY: RICHARD MITZMAN ARCHITECTS. BUILT BY: THE HIDDEN MODELSHOP) NFS
wood and brass
Richard Mitzman

804 DESIGN FOR A DOOR HANDLE SET NFS
sketch, wood mock-up, paper lamwate model and cast prototype
Eric Parry RA

805 THE SACRISTY, HOW TO KEEP A ROOM IN YOUR BOOKCASE NFS
model: plaster, wood, brass and leather
Konstantinos Elezis

806 SHOREDITCH CITY £ 500
plaster, ink, gold and bronze powder
Elena Tsolakis

807 ROBERT GORDON UNIVERSITY NFS
wood, plastic
Edward Cullinan RA

808 STRATEGIC ARMATURE DIAGRAM FOR A FUTURE PARIS   NFS
perspex
Lord Rogers of Riverside RA

809 SANTA MARIA DEL PIANTO UNDERGROUND STATION   NFS
ROOF: STRUCTURE DESIGN DEVELOPMENT MODEL
rapid prototype
Lord Rogers of Riverside RA

810 PLASTIC PROUVÉ, 2005   NFS
moulded plastic, bolts
Xin Yu

811 EMBODIED CONTOURS   £ 7,950
paper and prototype
Ben Cowd and Tobias Klein

812 V&A JEWELLERY GALLERY STAIR   NFS
model
Eva Jiricna RA

813 PAPER STRUCTURE EXPERIMENT 1   NFS
paper
Amelia Samways

814 ONE BLACKFRIARS ROAD 1:1000 SCALE CAST MODEL   NFS
DESCRIBING THE SCULPTURAL FORM OF DESIGN
cast pewter and clear polished acrylic
Ian Simpson Architects

815 FREYA'S CABIN (ARCHITECTURAL STUDY MODEL   NFS
AS PART OF 'FREYA AND ROBIN' PROJECT, KIELDER,
NORTHUMBERLAND)
plywood, acrylic, rods and nuts
Studio Weave

816 SPORTS CENTRE, THE KEYS QUINTA DO LAGO   NFS
(MODEL BY: SARAH BROMLEY)
mixed media
Walker Bushe Architects

817 LONDON HOTEL CONCEPT   NFS
model
Lifschutz Davidson Sandilands

818 HERMITAGE PLAZA PARIS: STUDY MODEL   NFS
perspex
Lord Foster of Thames Bank RA

819 INSIDE-OUT HOUSE   NFS
model: acid-etched brass, mdf, acrylic paint
Studio Weave

820 THE NEW STADIUM AT LANSDOWNE ROAD (SECTION)   NFS
model
Ben Vickery, HOK Sport Architecture

821 ELLIPTIC BRIDGE   NFS
brass, wood and aluminium
McMorran and Gatehouse Architects Ltd

822 HOUSE ABSTRACTION   NFS
wood
Stephenson Bell Architects

823 SYNERGY, HIERARCHY OF STRUCTURE AND   NFS
DAYLIGHT INTERACTION
nylon, selective lazer sintering
Denise Cloutt

824 ZAHA HADID ARCHITECTS. DENSITY STUDY,   NFS
KARTAL PENDIK MASTERPLAN, ISTANBUL, TURKEY
stl model
Zaha Hadid RA

825 ZAHA HADID ARCHITECTS. GRID STUDY,   NFS
KARTAL PENDIK MASTERPLAN, ISTANBUL, TURKEY
stl model
Zaha Hadid RA

826 ZAHA HADID ARCHITECTS. BLOCK STUDY,   NFS
KARTAL PENDIK MASTERPLAN, ISTANBUL, TURKEY
stl model, 3D printing
Zaha Hadid RA

827 ZAHA HADID ARCHITECTS. URBAN CALIGRAPHY,   NFS
KARTAL PENDIK MASTERPLAN, ISTANBUL, TURKEY
stl model, 3D printing
Zaha Hadid RA

828 **TRIBECA INFO BOX** £ 10,000
wood, perspex and card
Patrick Michell

829 **INNSCAPE, HOUSING PROJECT FOR INNSBRUCK,** £ 5,000
AUSTRIA
model
architektur.bn / Sasa Bradic, Ines Nizic

830 **AXING MiEs – SECTION** NFS
OR PLAN, DRAWING OR MODEL.
(TICK OR TREAT FOR MIES AND MiEs.)
wood, cardboard, ink and pencil
Heidi Lee

831 **BUNNY CLUB, QUEEN MARY'S GARDEN, NW1.** £ 20,000
card and paper
Studio 8 Architects

832 **GATEWAY GAMES: CONSTRUCTING THE MIES –** NFS
CIGAR & TEA TIMES
wood, tea leaves, plaster, chocolate and brass
Heidi Lee

833 **MAKING SPACE 1** £ 10,000
sketch model
Gordon Benson RA

834 **MAKING SPACE 2 (LEFT – MKI, RIGHT – MKVII)** £ 450
print
Gordon Benson RA
(edition of 20: £150 each)

835 **MAKING SPACE 3 (LEFT – MKII, RIGHT – MKV)** £ 450
print
Gordon Benson RA
(edition of 20: £150 each)

836 **MAKING SPACE 4 (LEFT – MK III, RIGHT – MKIV)** £ 450
print
Gordon Benson RA
(edition of 20: £150 each)

837 **SHELTER 55/02, FACTORY FILES (1:20)** NFS
selective laser sintering
Sixteen* (Makers)

848 NATIONAL OPERA STUDIO DESIGN STUDY　　£ 300
plaster, ink, and black paint
Elena Tsolakis

849 OFFICE BUILDING, MANCHESTER　　£ 1,500
acetate
William Alsop RA

850 MAISON DE LA PAIX, GENEVA (MODEL BY: A MODELS)　　NFS
model
Sanei Hopkins Architects

851 RECONSTRUCTING DUBLIN　　£ 750
digital print
Emily Lewith
(edition of 10: £500 each)

852 SCOTLAND'S HOME OF TOMORROW　　£ 250
etching
Ian Ritchie RA
(edition of 15: £200 each)

853 ARRANGEMENT　　£ 200
ink and digital
Marina Illum
(edition of 100: £100 each)

854 PONTOON DOCK BRIDGE　　NFS
acrylic
Weston Williamson

855 TO KNOW THE CAUSES OF THINGS, NEW INN PASSAGE,　　NFS
LONDON. ART/ARCHITECTURE INTERVENTION FOR
THE LONDON SCHOOL OF ECONOMICS (LSE)
card and string
Feix&Merlin Architects

856 KIT HOUSE　　NFS
model: wood and perspex
Eldridge Smerin Architects

857 FERRY TERMINAL, DUBAI　　NFS
card
Will Alsop RA

858 HARPER STREET NFS
foam board and digital print
Charles Holland, FAT

859 MARS £ 4,000
iron bucket, acrylic glass, adhesive dots
Norbert Brunner

860 VENUS £ 4,000
iron bucket, acrylic glass, adhesive dots
Norbert Brunner

861 LASER PLY TIMBER SURFACE NFS
plywood
Anahita Chouhan

862 CORNERSTONE ARTS BUILDING SPACE STUDY NFS
coloured resin, perspex and paper print
Dominic Williams

863 TRAVELLING LIGHT £ 8,000
acid etched and stainless steel
Piercy Conner Architects

864 UNIVERSITY OF AMSTERDAM, AMSTERDAM, HOLLAND NFS
perspex and wood
Allford Hall Monagan Morris

865 SHANGHAI EXPO NFS
architectural model
Marks Barfield Architects

866 DEPLOYABLE ROOF NFS
ply, mdf, metal rods, bolts
Ademola Abegunde

867 ZAHA HADID ARCHITECTS. OVERALL MASTERPLAN, NFS
KARTAL PENDIK MASTERPLAN, ISTANBUL, TURKEY
stl model
Zaha Hadid RA

868 MIDDLEHAVEN – CONCEPTS NFS
foam board and balsa wood
Charles Holland, FAT

869 SCHOOL OF ARCHITECTURE AT THE CHINESE UNIVERSITY NFS
OF HONG KONG
card and metal
Stephenson Bell Architects

870 STRATFORD TOWERS INITIAL MODEL NFS
wood off-cuts
Eric Parry RA

871 DREAMING OF A PROJECT £ 300
etching
Ian Ritchie RA
(edition of 20: £250 each)

872 GENEVA COMEDIE £ 250
etching
Ian Ritchie RA
(edition of 12: £200 each)

873 CHICHESTER CULTURAL OLYMPIAD £ 250
etching
Ian Ritchie RA
(edition of 12: £200 each)

874 110 THREE COLT STREET £ 250
etching
Ian Ritchie RA
(edition of 15: £200 each)

875 INTO THE SIDINGS £ 250
etching
Ian Ritchie RA
(edition of 12: £200 each)

876 SQUARE THE BLOCK £ 2,000
wood, card and felt tip
Richard Wilson RA

877 SLOUGH TRANSPORT INTERCHANGE NFS
plastic, spraypaint, perspex
Matthew Bedward (bblur Architecture)

878 ALLEN GARDENS FARMSTED, CHRISTCHURCH £ 3,000
(HOUSING PROJECT)
corten, perspex, timber
Chris Dyson

879 WE HAVE GREAT EXPECTATIONS, £ 750
CHARLES DICKENS PRIMARY SCHOOL, SOUTHWARK
card model
AOC Architecture

880 5 ALDERMANBURY SQUARE, LONDON EC2, SEQUENCE OF NFS
MODELS THROUGH THE DESIGN DEVELOPMENT, SCALE 1:500
mixed media
Eric Parry RA

881 NEW SPACES FOR THE ROYAL ACADEMY AT NFS
BURLINGTON GARDENS: GALLERY 8, ROOF VOID OFFICES
AND MEZZANINES, 2007-9 SECTIONS
digital print
Dannatt, Johnson Architects (Trevor Dannatt RA)

882 MEZZANINES AND BASEMENT OFFICES: NFS
NEW SPACES FOR THE ROYAL ACADEMY AT
BURLINGTON GARDENS, 2007
photographs
Dannatt, Johnson Architects (Trevor Dannatt RA)

883 GALLERY 8 AND ROOF VOID OFFICES: NEW SPACES NFS
FOR THE ROYAL ACADEMY AT BURLINGTON GARDENS
(UNDER CONSTRUCTION)
photographs
Dannatt, Johnson Architects (Trevor Dannatt RA)

884 TOP SECRET PAVILION, LONDON NFS
paper, wood, perspex and copper
Philip Gumuchdjian

885 PAST EXPERIMENTS NFS
card, wood, plastic
Edward Cullinan RA

886 OPIUM IS A SEASON £ 600
digital print on archival watercolour paper
Yaojen Chuang
(edition of 15: £500 each)

887 THE EUPHORIC FIELD £ 600
digital print on archival watercolour paper
Yaojen Chuang
(edition of 15: £500 each)

888 BAT SPIRAL NFS
mixed media
Friend and Company Architects

889 YACHT CLUB DE MONACO: MODEL NFS
timber plastic
Spencer de Grey RA

890 BASCULE BRIDGE NFS
architectural model
Lifschutz Davidson Sandilands

891 APRAKSIN DVOR MASTERPLAN NFS
acrylic, cast resin and etched stainless steel
Chris Wilkinson RA

892 I–HUB CONCEPT SKETCH 2 £ 225
pencil
Paul Koralek RA

893 I – HUB CONCEPT SKETCH 1 £ 225
pencil
Paul Koralek RA

894 PARC 1, SEOUL, KOREA NFS
foam board
Martha Schwartz Partners

895 PRIVATE RESIDENCE, ISLE OF WHITE. NFS
SECTIONAL MODEL, SCALE 1:50
plywood and cork
Michael Manser RA

896 VIENNA ECONOMICS UNIVERSITY: FORM STUDIES £ 3,000
foam on card
Sir Peter Cook RA and Gavin Robotham (CRAB)

897 BOX 7 (MAQUETTE FOR FULL SIZE WORK 225 x 330) £ 1,000
photographic print
Roderick Coyne

898 BOX 8 (MAQUETTE FOR FULL SIZE WORK 225 x 330)   £ 1,000
photographic print
Roderick Coyne

899 EEL NET BRIDGE   NFS
brass tube
Tim Lucas, Price & Myers LLP

900 SLIDING   £ 5,200
cardboard
Trine Olrik

901 RESONATING BODIES IN VISCOUS SPACE   £ 20,000
prototype, objet resin
Tobias Klein

902 EXPLODED VIEW OF THE EXPERIMENTAL MEDIA AND   NFS
PERFORMING ARTS CENTER; TROY, NEW YORK
computer-generated drawing
Sir Nicholas Grimshaw PRA

903 MURAL SEXTANT, CANVEY ISLAND, ESSEX   NFS
brass, perspex, stainless steel, etched copper
and spray paint
Kyle Buchanan

904 MAHARASHTRA CRICKET ASSOCATION   NFS
white sketch model
Sir Michael Hopkins RA

905 TIMBER OFFICE BUILDING, VICTORIA (SCALE 1:100)   £ 3,000
plywood, resin, brass
Patrick Lynch

906 SUNDIAL   NFS
architectural model
Stuart Walker

907 NIZHNY NOVGOROD WINTER SPORTS COMPLEX   NFS
acrylic and etched stainless steel
Chris Wilkinson RA

908 TRIBECA INFO BOX PAUILION   £ 5,000
architectural model
Alex Flint and David Shanks

909 HARROW FURTHER EDUCATION COLLEGE — NFS
mixed media
Sir Richard MacCormac RA

910 CROMWELL SQUARE — NFS
white card model, mdf base
Peter Barber Architects

911 VIENNA ECONOMICS UNIVERSITY ENTRANCE — £ 2,000
digital drawing
Sir Peter Cook RA and Gavin Robotham (CRAB)

912 LIBRARY ROOF GARDEN — £ 2,000
various
Sir Peter Cook RA and Gavin Robotham (CRAB)

913 HIDDEN CITY — £ 10,000
ink, gouache and watercolour
Sir Peter Cook RA

914 SALCOMBE MARINE HOTEL CONTEXTUAL MODEL 1:500 — NFS
perspex
Lord Rogers of Riverside RA

915 LIBRARY, ADMINISTRATION BUILDING AND CONGRESS CENTRE, UNIVERSITY TOMAS BATA, ZLIN — NFS
duratrans on lightbox
Eva Jiricna RA

916 WILLIAM AND JUDITH BOLLINGER JEWELLERY GALLERY, VICTORIA AND ALBERT MUSEUM — NFS
duratrans on lightbox
Eva Jiricna RA

917 OCEAN TERMINAL, SOUTHAMPTON. SECTION THROUGH NEW TERMINAL BUILDING FOR 4,000 PASSENGER CAPACITY CRUISE SHIPS, SCALE 1:100 — NFS
white acrylic
Michael Manser RA

918 SALCOMBE MARINE HOTEL SECTIONAL MODEL 1:100 — NFS
perspex
Lord Rogers of Riverside RA

919 LONG SECTION OF THE BRITISH MUSEUM NFS
digital print on paper
Lord Rogers of Riverside RA

920 OXFORD QUADRANGLE (ARTIST: PETER HULL) £ 6,000
ink on watercolour paper
Sir Richard MacCormac RA
(edition of 50: £200 each)

921 A FUTURE FOR LETCHWORTH NFS
ink and graphite
Edward Cullinan RA

922 SECTION THROUGH THE EAST WING, NFS
THE NEUES MUSEUM, MUSEUM ISLAND, BERLIN
mixed media print on canvas, mounted on foamcore
David Chipperfield RA

923 SECTION THROUGH THE EGYPTIAN AND GREEK NFS
COURTYARDS, THE NEUES MUESUM,
MUSEUM ISLAND, BERLIN
mixed media print on canvas, mounted on foamcore
David Chipperfield RA

924 SECTION THROUGH THE WEST WING, NFS
THE NEUES MUSEUM, MUSEUM ISLAND, BERLIN
mixed media print on canvas, mounted on foamcore
David Chipperfield RA

925 WEST ELEVATION, THE NEUES MUSEUM, NFS
MUSEUM ISLAND, BERLIN
mixed media print on canvas, mounted on foamcore
David Chipperfield RA

926 EAST ELEVATION, THE NEUES MUSEUM, NFS
MUSEUM ISLAND, BERLIN
mixed media print on canvas, mounted on foamcore
David Chipperfield RA

927 FAUSTINO WINERY SPAIN NFS
timber plastic
Lord Foster of Thames Bank RA

928 REMODULATED ENVIRONMENT £ 47,950
ply and pine wood
Alexander Hills

---

929 PARAMETRIC URBANISM III: HOUSING PROPOSAL £ 3,000
FOR NEW YORK
piano wire, mdf, perspex, polyurethane foam
Team Shampoo

---

930 BMCE BANK BRANCHES MOROCCO: STUDY MODELS NFS
paper card 3d powder print
Spencer de Grey RA

---

931 CANADA WATER LIBRARY NFS
foamboard
Piers Gough RA

---

932 DEVELOPMENT OVER CANARY WHARF CROSSRAIL NFS
STATION: MODEL
3D powder print sls
Spencer de Grey RA

---

933 EXPLODED CONSTRUCTION AND SPATIAL STUDY OF NFS
ENVIRONMENTAL RESOURCE CLASSROOM, EBBW VALE
wood, plastic and metal model
Design Research Unit Wales

---

934 ELIZABETHAN DRESS £ 10,000
aluminium, abs and netting
Philippa Downes, Sarah Milburn, Julio Alves and
Louise Fricker

---

935 CASTELLIERO £ 8,625
swarovski crystal and mixed media
Nigel Coates

---

936 WASTE £ 9,500
plywood, planting (earth), plastic, timber,
stainless steel, glass, granite, paper, card
Lucy Tauber

937	**HILLSIDE, FROM A PERSIAN RUG** *oil* Adrian Berg RA	£ 6,000
938	**BENGAL BIRDS** *oil* Adrian Berg RA	£ 6,000
939	**A PATH AND TREE** *oil and coloured pencil on canvas* Rose Wylie	£ 9,000
940	**SMARTIES** *oil on board* Neal Jones	£ 1,600
941	**ODDBALLS** *oil on board* Neal Jones	£ 1,600
942	**LOST IN THE FREE TIME, 2009** *acrylic* Bill Henderson	£ 6,500
943	**ON THE FLOOR** *oil* Kathleen Thompson	£ 3,500
944	**THE TIPPING POINT** *oil and charcoal on linen* Jeffrey Dennis	£ 2,400
945	**FULL IMMERSION** *acrylic* Luciana Meazza	£ 2,500

946 INVISIBLE LIVES £ 7,500
acrylic on linen
C Morey de Morand

947 DRAGGING 2004 – 2007 £ 3,800
acrylic and collage on board
Anthony Whishaw RA

948 INTERIOR WITH FIGURE 2004 – 2008 £ 4,250
acrylic and collage on board
Anthony Whishaw RA

949 CACTUS 1 £ 1,700
acrylic
Peter Arscott

950 HABITAT WEST OF CHINA £ 6,500
oil
Adrian Berg RA

951 LOOKING EAST #1 £ 950
watercolour on rice straw paper
Maurice Cockrill RA

952 RECALL, LOST GARDEN £ 8,750
oil on board
Sonia Lawson RA

953 BLUE RIDER £ 6,850
oil on board
Sonia Lawson RA

954 NIGHT DRIVE £ 14,700
oil
Sonia Lawson RA

955 LOOKING EAST #6 £ 950
watercolour on rice straw paper
Maurice Cockrill RA

956 BEACH FIGURE II £ 3,250
monotype
Ivor Abrahams RA

957 LA VILLANEUVETTE £ 2,450
mixed media
Ivor Abrahams RA

958 LAVENDER BORDER £ 2,525
flock fibre on screenprint
Ivor Abrahams RA

959 FLOWER BED £ 2,000
giclée
Ivor Abrahams RA
(edition of 20, framed: £2,000 each)

960 DANCER E £ 2,550
cut-out card
Ivor Abrahams RA

961 BEACH FIGURE I £ 3,250
monotype
Ivor Abrahams RA

962 SPLIT INFINITIVE 6 £ 3,500
acrylic
Flavia Irwin RA

963 SPLIT INFINITIVE 8 £ 3,500
acrylic
Flavia Irwin RA

964 THE OLD LEAD INTO WAKEHURST PLACE £ 15,000
oil
Adrian Berg RA

965 FROM THE CENTRE OF A PERSIAN RUG £ 5,000
oil
Adrian Berg RA

966 FISHIING, FROM A BENGAL RUG £ 6,000
oil
Adrian Berg RA

967 ROUNDELAY £ 5,700
acrylic
Tricia Gillman

968 COMMON SENSE £ 17,000
acrylic
Gerard Hemsworth

969 IN THE NIGHT, AVIGNON £ 7,500
acrylic
Julie Held

970 69 CAMBERWELL GROVE, OR SO IT SEEMED £ 900
archival giclée print on canvas
Kevin O'Keefe
(edition of 30: £750 each)

971 JAPANESE LANDSCAPE £ 1,250
woodcut
Morgan Doyle
(edition of 10: £950 each)

972 FLOOR AND DOG £ 3,500
oil on canvas
Kathleen Thompson

973 NO RETURN 2, 2008 £ 8,500
acrylic
John Loker

974 OPEN ARMS £ 8,400
oil
Lisa Wright

975 FAINT ECHOES £ 3,500
acrylic
Gus Cummins RA

976 BUCOLIC HIPPY PAINTING 2 £ 3,000
oil on linen
Clyde Hopkins

977 SPIDERMAN AND THE BLACK ORCHID £ 7,000
acrylic, alkyd, plastic glitter and chalk on canvas
Alex Ramsay

978 VERTIGO I 2004 – 2007 £ 2,800
acrylic
Anthony Whishaw RA

979	**STAINED WITH A THOUSAND FIRES BY OCEAN SUNS** *oil and mixed media* Zheni Warner	£ 4,500
980	**SCHEMA** *ink on paper* Juliette Losq	£ 3,500
981	**THERE WAS A CHILD WENT FORTH EVERYDAY** *enamelled steel* Randy Klein	£ 3,000
982	**T. CIRCLE** *news papers* Yoshimi Kihara	£ 3,600
983	**BLACK 2008** *bronze* Nicola Hicks (edition of 3: £100,000 each)	NFS
984	**MEDITATION / BREATH 2008** *stainless steel and copper* John Gibbons	£ 5,500
985	**SHIFT NO. 10** *stone and steel* Maurice Agis	£ 5,000
986	**BETWEEN GREEN** *painted g.r.p. and rag paper* Terry New (edition of 10: £1,800 each)	£ 1,800
987	**ANGOULEME II** *mild steel, forged constructed and welded* Katherine Gili	£ 18,500

---

988 ANDALUSIA £ 50,000
mixed media on canvas
Barbara Rae RA

---

989 5 COLOUR PAINTING 1, 2009 £ 1,185
acrylic paint on birch faced plywood
Nigel O'Neill

---

990 TUSK £ 1,800
household paint
Mary Ramsden

---

991 DETOUR £ 15,000
acrylic
Paul Tonkin

---

992 NEGATIVE SPACE, SOUTH BANK, NO. 1 £ 2,200
oil
Steve McConaghy

---

993 NEGATIVE SPACE, SOUTH BANK, NO. 2 £ 2,200
oil
Steve McConaghy

---

994 CROSS-HARBOUR SOUND £ 3,500
mixed media on wood
Janet Nathan

---

995 FLUX £ 10,000
mixed media on canvas
Livia Paola Gorresio

---

996 RIPE CORN NEAR ST. MARGARET'S (OTTY BOTTOM) £ 7,200
oil
George Rowlett

997	**A BRIDGE IN KYOTO 2008** *oil and collage on board* Trevor Sutton	£ 9,000
998	**DAYS END** *acrylic* Sheila Girling	£ 10,000
999	**ICE FIELD, 2009** *oil* Carol Robertson	£ 3,500
1000	**STUNTS** *oil on wood* David Small	£ 1,200
1001	**SHADOW LOVE** *gouache on paper* Mick Owens	£ 750
1002	**WITHOUT A SHADOW, 2009** *oil* Carol Robertson	£ 10,000
1003	**MIND HORIZON, 5-6-07** *acrylic on cotton* John Hoyland RA	NFS
1004	**FIGURE IN A LANDSCAPE** *oil* Susie Hamilton	£ 7,000
1005	**LOUSE POINT HOMAGE, 1997** *oil* Gary Wragg	£ 14,000
1006	**PLASTIC ELEMENTS** *oil and mixed media on canvas* Anthony Francis	£ 5,800
1007	**CREATING SPACE** *gloss on canvas* Donna White	£ 3,000

1008 HAVANA £ 10,000
acrylic
John Holden

1009 CLEARING £ 450
oil
Paula Stanley

1010 MARIN £ 3,500
acrylic
Gina Medcalf

1011 GARDEN 05 £ 985
acrylic on ply
Peter Griffiths

1012 GNOISSIENNE £ 2,000
oil on paper
Hannah Birkett

1013 SUNRISE £ 17,000
oil
James Robertson RSA

1014 LIGHT OF SUMMER £ 5,750
mixed media on wood
Kenneth Draper RA

1015 DEEP WATERS £ 4,250
mixed media on paper
Kenneth Draper RA

1016 AUTUMN'S PROMISE £ 4,750
mixed media on wood
Kenneth Draper RA

1017 ENCLAVE £ 5,250
paste on paper
Kenneth Draper RA

1018 HEAVEN'S BREATH £ 3,500
mixed media on paper
Kenneth Draper RA

1019 RISING SEA £ 2,900
steel
Guy Thomas

1020 ERL-KING (2009) £ 450,000
steel
Sir Anthony Caro RA

1021 SCULPTURE OF VAN GOGH AFTER SELF £ 8,000
PORTRAIT OF 1887
jesmonite
John Dean
(edition of 7: £8,000 each)

1022 DECONSTRUCTING VELAZQUEZ £ 22,425
*artist's vector drawing controlled by bespoke
software on customized computer with lcd screen*
Michael Craig-Martin RA
(edition of 10: £22,425 each)

1023 FROM A PLANET £ 3,600
digital print on canvas with dissolved ink
Jane Ward

1024 ASCENSION £ 800
digital print mounted on aluminium
John Lawrence
(edition of 5: £800 each)

1025 JtB SERIES £ 2,950
mixed media on paper
Abdul Hakim Onitolo

1026 GENERAL BROWNING MOTH CLUB, HACKNEY £ 2,938
c-type print
Bridget Smith
(edition of 6: £2,500 each)

1027 CORA £ 1,200
photography
Inez de Coo
(edition of 3: £1,000 each)

1028 LUCKYLUCKYDICE.COM £ 600
digital archival print
James Howard
(edition of 15: £500 each)

1029 LONDON SERIES NO. 1 £ 950
photograph
Louise Carreck
(edition of 7: £750 each)

1030 DOOR £ 600
photographic print
Jonathan Gales & Claire Pepper
(edition of 10: £450 each)

1031 LONDON £ 1,540
digital print on photographic paper
Julio Brujis
(edition of 14: £1,200 each)

1032 INSEPARABLE £ 850
lambda photographic print
Helen Sear
(edition of 25: £700 each)

1033 BIRD 2 £ 1,553
photograph
Elizabeth Zeschin
(edition of 25: £1,437 each)

1034 GUANGZHOU ZOO 2 £ 3,500
lambda print
Kurt Tong
(edition of 5: £3,000 each)

1035 RORSCHACH SERIES, POOL SIDE, MV £ 550
digital print
Terry New
(edition of 20: £320 each)

1036 SHALLOW WATER £ 250
giclée photographic print on watercolour paper
Victoria White
(edition of 10: £200 each)

1037 EXPLOSION 2 £ 1,350
lambda print, mounted on aluminium
Joschi Herczeg
(edition of 10: £950 each)

1038 A MESSAGE FROM THE BEARS £ 195
lambda print of scanned photographic film
Martin Wilson
(edition of 250: £117 each)

1039 TOP'N TAIL £ 300
inkjet print
Miyako Narita
(edition of 30: £270 each)

1040 BALCONY IN FOG, VENICE £ 625
digital c-type photograph
Guy Sargent

1041 PREDATOR £ 25,000
postcard collage
David Mach RA

1042 URIEL £ 190
3-dimensional print
Tom Lomax
(edition of 30: £170 each)

1043 RAPHAEL £ 190
3-dimensional print
Tom Lomax
(edition of 30: £170 each)

1044 LEIGHTON AND SHE II £ 800
original digital print
Guler Ates
(edition of 10: £650 each)

1045 CAMOUFLAGE FRIGHT WIG Editions are available for sale
BLUE AND BRONZE ON PINK
silkscreen on Somerset satin 410 gsm
Gavin Turk
(edition of 40: £2,300 each)

1046 BADLANDS, ALBERTA £ 350
digital print on watercolour paper
Edward Bowman
(edition of 40: £250 each)

1047 UNTITLED 2 £ 600
photographic print
Dzenana Hozic
(edition of 5: £400 each)

1048 THE WORLD TAKES OVER £ 530
lambda c-type print
Carina Traberg
(edition of 30: £330 each)

1049 LOUNGE OF FORMER SANITORIUM, £ 3,000
SLUDYANKA, RUSSIA
photograph
Simon Roberts
(edition of 6: £2,500 each)

1050 UNTITLED, 2003 £ 250
c-type print
Natalia Calvocoressi
(edition of 15: £200 each)

1051 UNTITLED, FROM THE SERIES 'OTHER PLACES' £ 600
photographic print
Alana Lake
(edition of 8: £400 each)

1052 GOYAN TUMULT £ 220
digital image-archival print
Geoffrey Stocker
(edition of 40: £140 each)

1053 EXCAVATIONS £ 800
digital print
Paige Sinkler
(edition of 30: £500 each)

1054 BERLIN CATHEDRAL £ 3,000
lightjet print perspex mounted
Tom Leighton
(edition of 5: £3,000 each)

1055 DARK SKY £ 675
inkjet photograph
Jean Macalpine
(edition of 25: £525 each)

1056 FARM, BAGN, 2007 *giclée print* Michael Bodiam (edition of 15: £275 each)	£ 715
1057 ANGUS *archival print* Maciej Urbanek (edition of 21: £680 each)	£ 780
1058 ISLE OF MORT, 2008 *screenprint and archival ink jet* Stephen Walter (edition of 50: £805 each)	£ 990
1059 LILY COLE, 2009 *c-type photograph* Gillian Wearing RA (edition of 175)	£ 630
1060 WASTED YOUTH (25 ASHBOURNE AVE) *colour photograph* Petros Chrisostomou (edition of 5: £3,000 each)	£ 3,500
1061 JUBILEE OPERATIONS #1, KALGOORLIE, WESTERN AUSTRALIA 2007 *chromogenic colour print* Edward Burtynsky (edition of 6: £14,500 each)	£ 15,500
1062 TAXIS CROSS THE FROZEN LENA RIVER, YAKUTSK, RUSSIA *photograph* Simon Roberts (edition of 6: £4,000 each)	£ 4,500
1063 TO HAVE AND TO HOLD FROM THIS DAY FORWARD Paul Brooking (edition of 10: £800 each)	£ 1,000
1064 PLASTIC CUPS *digital c-type print in reverse mounted perpex* Nicky Walsh (edition of 10: £400 each)	£ 700

1065 AVATAR NO. 2　　　　　　　　　　　　　　　　£ 700
digital duotoned lithograph
Rhys Himsworth
(edition of 25: £450 each)

1066 AVATAR NO. 1　　　　　　　　　　　　　　　　£ 700
digital duotoned lithograph
Rhys Himsworth
(edition of 25: £450 each)

1067 VARANASI ROOFTOPS　　　　　　　　　　　　£ 4,500
archival pigment ink photograph
Tim Hall
(edition of 5: £3,750 each)

1068 METAL DETECTOR FINDS, LEAD INDIAN AND SOLDIERS　£ 1,345
*from a series of 6 archival inkjet prints presented in
individual folders*
Cornelia Parker
(edition of 30: £966 each)

1069 INBETWEEN　　　　　　　　　　　　　　　　£ 2,400
lambda print mounted on aluminium
Joc, Jon & Josch
(edition of 5: £1,800 each)

1070 MISS BULL AS ALCHAMIA EXAMINES THE　　　£ 1,900
**ALCHEMISTIC QUOTE, 'MARRIAGE GUM WITH GUM
IN TRUE MARRIAGE'**
c–type
Stine Ljungdalh
(edition of 5: £1,800 each)

1071 DUST BREEDING　　　　　　　　　　　　　　£ 1,750
photo work
Nigel Rolfe
(edition of 10: £1,450 each)

1072 PARADISE LOST　　　　　　　　　　　　　　£ 790
archival digital print
Barton Hargreaves
(edition of 8: £600 each)

1073 VIEW FROM MY KITCHEN WINDOW £ 2,415
continuous computer animation on an lcd screen,
silver powder-coated metal surround
Julian Opie
(edition of 200: £2,415 each)

1074 JUST SUCH AN EXIT AS THIS £ 750
digital print on archival fine art paper, lightbox
Alex Knell
(edition of 3: £400 each)

1075 ALTER EGO – PRIMUS INTER PARES £ 1,595
3-ply duratrans, 4-ply plexiglass, lightbox
Bernard Bowers
(edition of 16: £1,595 each)

1076 A TO ZED £ 2,000
mixed media
Steve Rosenthal

1077 SPANISH PLAYGROUND £ 950
giclée archival print
Max Forsythe
(edition of 25: £750 each)

1078 TAKING LIBERTIES £ 1,800
c-type print
Liane Lang
(edition of 5: £1,600 each)

1079 BATHERS, YIBIN, SICHUAN 2007 £ 7,000
chromogenic colour print
Nadav Kander
(edition of 5: £6,250 each)

1080 NORTH LONDON BEE KEEPERS ASSOCIATION, £ 2,938
HIGHGATE
c-type print
Bridget Smith
(edition of 6: £2,500 each)

1081 MAKING SPACE – 1 UNINTERRUPTED £ 2,500
archival giclée print mounted on aluminium
Vanja Karas
(edition of 50: £1,200 each)

1082 AN ERODED HISTORY OF THE LOWER DEPTHS VOL. II £ 1,250
archival inkjet and silkscreen print
Paul Haydock-Wilson
(edition of 3: £850 each)

1083 ESSAOUIRA STREET £ 245
c-type print
Dawn Bowery
(edition of 100: £180 each)

1084 TORNADO £ 600
archival digital print
Suzanne Moxhay
(edition of 10: £475 each)

1085 NEW YEARS DAY, EDINBURGH 2006 £ 450
c-type print
Natalia Calvocoressi
(edition of 10: £390 each)

1086 UNTITLED, FROM A SERIES £ 515
'MAKING WAY FOR THE GAMES'
giclée print
Brijesh Patel
(edition of 5: £415 each)

1087 MEDITATION / ENTER 2008 £ 7,500
stainless steel and copper
John Gibbons

1088 ROTA-CARVE £ 4,000
steel, plaster, wood
James Capper

1089 SAMPLE ON EXAMPLE £ 850
fimo, rubber band, souvenir bust
Guy Holder

1090 DRUMMER Editions available for sale
bronze
Jock McFadyen
(edition of 8: £28,750 each)

1091 THE WINNERSH TRIANGLE £ 500
digital animation
David Theobald
(edition of 6: £500 each)

1092 BURST© £ 3,000
digital video
David Edwin Marchant
(edition of 5: £3,000 each)

LECTURE ROOM

1093	**SNOW SCENE** *oil on board* Ben Levene RA	£ 6,500
1094	**AUTUMN WITH POPLAR FROM STUDIO WINDOW** *oil on board* Ben Levene RA	£ 4,500
1095	**THE BEACH, WALBERSWICK** *oil* William Bowyer RA	£ 8,000
1096	**MOORE'S THREE POINTS** *watercolour* Shanti Panchal	£ 7,500
1097	**STORMY WEATHER AFTER THE RAIN** *oil on board* Ben Levene RA	£ 6,500
1098	**LATE AUGUST, HEREFORDSHIRE** *oil* Ben Levene RA	£ 7,500
1099	**MORNING LIGHT EFFECT S. GIORGIO MAGGIORE** *oil* Ken Howard RA	£ 20,000
1100	**VENETIAN INTERIOR REFLECTION EFFECT 09** *oil* Ken Howard RA	£ 33,000
1101	**PURPLE FLOCK** *oil on linen* Shani Rhys-James	£ 25,875

1102 CALDY ISLAND £ 19,000
oil
Philip Sutton RA

1103 'AND MID THESE DANCING ROCKS AT ONCE AND EVER' £ 15,000
oil
Anthony Eyton RA

1104 TWO GOTHS IN A CAFE £ 1,200
oil on card
Michael Kirkbride

1105 MEMORY PICTURE, THE EMERGENCY ROOM £ 3,200
watercolour
Leonard Rosoman RA

1106 20TH STREET MILONGA £ 6,250
watercolour
David Remfry RA

1107 F.M. SHOES £ 6,250
watercolour and graphite
David Remfry RA

1108 CROSSING THE SQUARE IN THE SNOW I £ 3,450
monotype on paper
Bill Jacklin RA

1109 INTO THE SEA AT NIGHT I £ 3,450
monotype on paper
Bill Jacklin RA

1110 TALL MAN AVOIDING A DRUNKEN WOMAN £ 1,200
oil on card
Michael Kirkbride

1111 METROPOLIS £ 10,850
acrylic
P J Crook

1112 QUANTOCK FIGURE £ 5,000
oil
David Imms

1113 THE ROAD £ 12,000
acrylic
John Wragg RA

1114 NADIA £ 18,500
oil
Ishbel Myerscough

1115 VENETIAN OCTET £ 20,000
oil
Ken Howard RA

1116 STRAND ON THE GREEN £ 12,500
oil
William Bowyer RA

1117 WATERMANS £ 8,000
oil
William Bowyer RA

1118 UNTITLED £ 5,500
oil on copper
Nadia Hebson

1119 SILENT REFLECTION £ 8,500
oil on linen
George Underwood

1120 POMEGRANATES, MELONS AND SILK RIBBON £ 18,500
oil
Dame Elizabeth Blackadder RA

1121 EVENING'S WATER POLO £ 1,800
oil
Charles Williams

1122 THE READER £ 1,800
oil
Charles Williams

1123 PARKA £ 1,700
oil on paper
Anna Gardiner

1124 LEARNING TO SWIM £ 5,000
oil
Sasha Bowles

1125 PROSPECT OF WHITBY £ 7,900
acrylic
Cyril Croucher

1126 PORTRAIT OF THE ARTIST AS A YOUNG CHILD (II) £ 10,500
acrylic
June Collier

1127 THERE'S A STORM COMING £ 5,550
oil
Ursula McCannell

1128 COLLEEN AND HER BOY (I) £ 5,000
oil
Ursula McCannell

1129 SAFE PASSAGE £ 12,000
oil
Eileen Cooper RA

1130 ENCHANTMENT £ 8,000
oil
Eileen Cooper RA

1131 AUTUMN GRASSES £ 16,000
oil
Anthony Eyton RA

1132 UPPER MALL, HAMMERSMITH £ 12,000
oil
William Bowyer RA

1133 TWO WOMEN DRINKING CHAMPAGNE £ 37,375
oil
David Inshaw

1134 ON TOP OF IT ALL £ 4,300
oil
Sasha Bowles

1135	**BRIGHT REWARD** *oil* John Bellany RA	£ 30,000
1136	**RAIN EFFECT S. MARCO 09** *oil* Ken Howard RA	£ 33,000
1137	**SPRING STUDIO** *oil* Anthony Eyton RA	£ 18,000
1138	**BEEHIVES, LITTLE SPARTA** *oil and charcoal on panel* Eileen Hogan	£ 18,000
1139	**MENORCA** *oil* Derek Balmer	£ 6,850
1140	**MCDONALD'S, REGENT STREET** *pastel* Anthony Eyton RA	£ 9,500
1141	**FIGS** *oil* Mary Fedden RA	£ 18,000
1142	**FRUIT** *oil* Mary Fedden RA	£ 18,000
1143	**PICKING FLOWERS** *oil* Mary Fedden RA	£ 18,000
1144	**OYSTERS, CRAB AND SEA URCHIN** *oil* Dame Elizabeth Blackadder RA	£ 11,000
1145	**LE MONT ST. MICHEL** *watercolour* Carey Clarke	£ 7,500

1168 ST MICHAEL'S MOUNT, MOONSET £ 15,000
oil on board
Frederick Cuming RA

1169 TENNYSON DOWN AND RAINBOW £ 15,000
oil on board
Frederick Cuming RA

1170 FISHERS IN THE SNOW £ 100,000
oil
John Bellany RA

1171 FROM BROOKLYN TO MANHATTAN £ 12,000
watercolour and ink
Chris Orr RA

1172 PICTURES FROM STORYVILLE £ 24,000
graphite and watercolour
David Remfry RA

1173 SAFE £ 6,000
oil on linen
Jennifer McRae

1174 SELF PORTRAIT WITH FANTIN LATOUR £ 35,000
oil
Ken Howard RA

1175 BLUE BED AND CUSHION £ 4,500
acrylic
David Tindle RA

1176 STILL LIFE ON FRUIT TRAY £ 5,500
egg tempera
David Tindle RA

1177 EYESHADE £ 6,000
egg tempera
David Tindle RA

1178 STUDIO VIEW £ 4,500
oil on panel
Peter Layzell

1179	**CITYSCAPE**	£ 17,000
	oil	
	Donald Hamilton Fraser RA	

1180	**AMARYLLIS AND INDIAN EMBROIDERED SILK BAG**	£ 24,000
	oil	
	Dame Elizabeth Blackadder RA	

1181	**FAMILY IN THE COUNTRYSIDE**	£ 800
	oil	
	Carl Randall	

1182	**GIRL IN A SMALL NORTHERN JAPANESE TOWN**	£ 1,000
	oil	
	Carl Randall	

1183	**IN MEMORY OF A LOST VIOLIN**	£ 4,300
	charcoal	
	Sonia Lawson RA	

1184	**HORNBY TRAIN GAME**	NFS
	oil	
	Mick Rooney RA	

1185	**IRIS**	£ 2,500
	acrylic	
	David Tindle RA	

1186	**WILLOW ROSE BUCKLE**	£ 2,250
	oil	
	Mary Carter	

1187	**FRIDAY NIGHT GIRLS**	£ 1,900
	oil on board	
	Susan Bower	

1188	**STUDIO, JAPANESE PLATE AND CHINCHERINCHEES**	£ 35,000
	oil	
	Dame Elizabeth Blackadder RA	

1189	**TO REMAIN**	£ 5,950
	oil	
	Mick Rooney RA	

1190	LUNAR HORNPIPE	£ 5,950
	oil	
	Mick Rooney RA	

1191	INDOOR PURSUITS	£ 5,950
	oil	
	Mick Rooney RA	

1192	BY THE SEA	£ 15,000
	egg tempera	
	David Tindle RA	

1193	SILVER	£ 25,000
	postcard collage	
	David Mach RA	

1194	DORA, SNOW IN KENSINGTON GARDENS	£ 33,000
	oil	
	Ken Howard RA	

1195	EARTH SPACE–FALLEN BRANCHES–INNER WOOD–PEMBROKESHIRE	£ 995
	oil	
	Maurice Sheppard	

1196	BEACH SCENE 2009	£ 1,950
	oil on panel	
	Alfred Stockham	

1197	THE BEDROOM WINDOW	£ 1,950
	oil	
	Eric Seeley	

1198	PIER, LOW TIDE 2009	£ 1,950
	oil on panel	
	Alfred Stockham	

1199	APHRODITE INHERITANCE	£ 1,900
	watercolour and gold leaf on paper	
	Linda Sutton	

1200	IRAQ: THE SOUND OF YOUR SILENCE	*
	carved limewood	
	Michael Sandle RA	

Refer to Sales Desk

1201 CONVERSATION WITH DISTANT STONES £ 39,100
granite, gneiss, sandstone, slate and whin
John Maine RA

1202 COMPOSITION STUDY, LANDSCAPE £ 5,000
bronze
Christopher Le Brun RA
(edition of 6: £5,000 each)

1203 PAINTED TOWER £ 6,000
painted bronze
Christopher Le Brun RA

1204 COMPOSITION STUDY, TOWER £ 5,000
bronze
Christopher Le Brun RA
(edition of 6: £5,000 each)

1205 COMPOSITION WITH CIRCLES £ 5,000
bronze
Christopher Le Brun RA
(edition of 8: £5,000 each)

1206 CITY WING, MAQUETTE FOR THE TEN METRE BRONZE £ 7,000
AT 125 OLD BROAD STREET, THE CITY OF LONDON
bronze
Christopher Le Brun RA
(edition of 6: £7,000 each)

CENTRAL HALL

1207	**EXPLORING THE COUNTRY (WALES) NO.3** *watercolour* Leonard Rosoman RA	£ 3,200
1208	**SELF PORTRAIT** *watercolour* Leonard Rosoman RA	£ 3,800
1209	**FALLING CHRISTMAS TREE** *acrylic* Leonard Rosoman RA	£ 8,500
1210	**LOOKER** *postcard collage* David Mach RA	£ 25,000
1211	**ENTRANCE TO THE GARDEN** *oil* William Bowyer RA	£ 8,000
1212	**CHISWICK HOUSE** *oil* William Bowyer RA	£ 10,000
1213	**ST. MICHAEL'S MOUNT** *screenprint* Donald Hamilton Fraser RA (edition of 175: £495 each)	£ 640
1214	**KINLOCHBERVIE RED SKY** *screenprint* Donald Hamilton Fraser RA (edition of 175: £495 each)	£ 640
1215	**FISHERMENS LIFE** *oil* John Bellany RA	£ 30,000

1216 SEATED QUEEN £ 400
giclée print
Ralph Brown RA
(edition of 35: £390 each)

1217 SEATED MAN £ 400
giclée print
Ralph Brown RA
(edition of 35: £390 each)

1218 GIRL IN THE WIND £ 400
giclée print
Ralph Brown RA
(edition of 35: £390 each)

1219 BIRTH OF ICARUS, 1998 £ 15,000
oil
The Late Jean Cooke RA

1220 GARDEN IN SPRINGTIME, c. 1990 £ 12,000
oil on board
The Late Jean Cooke RA

1221 PORTRAIT OF JOHN BRATBY SEATED, c. 1970 £ 18,000
oil
The Late Jean Cooke RA

1222 SOFAS GALORE, c. 1980 £ 24,000
oil
The Late Jean Cooke RA

1223 JAMAIS JE NE PLEURE ET JAMAIS JE NE RIS NFS
oil
The Late Jean Cooke RA

1224 BABY IN CRADLE, c. 1960 £ 8,000
oil on panel
The Late Jean Cooke RA

1225 SPRINGTIME, 2009 £ 12,000
oil
Frederick Gore RA

1226 CESERANA, TUSCANY £ 7,500
oil
John Bellany RA

1227	**DODONA WINDY DAY**	£ 9,000
	oil on board	
	Donald Hamilton Fraser RA	

1228	**THE MONUMENT AND RIVERSIDE BUILDINGS**	£ 5,500
	pastel	
	Anthony Eyton RA	

1229	**THE BUNDT, SHANGHAI**	£ 6,000
	oil	
	John Bellany RA	

1230	**THE TEA BREAK, REMEMBER PASADENA!**	£ 21,850
	oil	
	Anthony Green RA	

1231	**BECKETT AGAIN**	£ 9,750
	oil on palettes	
	Tom Phillips RA	

1232	**SPLIT INFINITIVE 5**	£ 2,000
	pencil on paper	
	Flavia Irwin RA	

1233	**WING**	£ 10,000
	plaster	
	Christopher Le Brun RA	
	(edition of 6: £10,000 each)	

1234	**TULIPS**	£ 22,000
	oil	
	Elizabeth Blackadder RA	

1235	**SEPTEMBER**	£ 15,000
	oil	
	Frederick Gore RA	

1236	**THE BRIDGE, RAINFOREST, EDEN**	£ 900
	screenprint	
	Anthony Eyton RA	
	(edition of 30: £740 each)	

1237	**OH, WILD WEST WIND, 2008**	£ 12,000
	oil	
	Frederick Gore RA	

1238 LOOKING THROUGH THE MIRROR £ 9,000
oil on board
Ben Levene RA

1239 TEASER £ 25,000
postcard collage
David Mach RA

1240 EXPLORING THE COUNTRY (WALES) NO. 2 £ 3,200
watercolour
Leonard Rosoman RA

1241 EXPLORING THE COUNTRY (WALES) NO. 1 £ 3,200
watercolour
Leonard Rosoman RA

1242 VIEW FROM LITTLE RACKWAY £ 6,000
oil on board
Ben Levene RA

1243 FIGURE/HEAD £ 23,000
aluminium
Ralph Brown RA
(edition of 7: £23,000 each)

1244 DIVERS £ 11,500
bronze
Ralph Brown RA
(edition of 8: £11,500 each)

1245 QUEEN 2008 £ 92,000
bronze
Ralph Brown RA
(edition of 5: £92,000 each)

1246 MOON GOLD HARE, 2008 NFS
bronze and gilded bronze
Barry Flanagan RA
(edition of 8)

1247 SAINT BARTHOLOMEW, EXQUISITE PAIN NFS
silver
Damien Hirst
(edition of 3)

1248 AUTOMATON *
audio visual
Sean Dower
(edition of 5)

1249 WEBERN FACE DANCE *
audio visual
Brian Routh

1250 GLOSS *
audio visual
Matt Calderwood

1251 AUTOMOTIVE ACTION PAINTING (FUNDED BY FILM AND *
VIDEO UMBRELLA AND UK FILM COUNCIL)
audio visual
George Barber

1252 SPIN DOGTOR *
audio visual
Miyako Narita
(edition of 50)

1253 SURPRISE NFS
audio visual
Ben Dodd

1254 OM *
audio visual
John Smith

1255 TRANSLATIONS *
audio visual
Rachel Cohen

1256 RICKSHAW NO. 1 (TWO TIMES THREE) NFS
audio visual
Rachel Lowe

* Refer to Sales Desk

1257 THERE IS NO SELF   *
audio visual
Martin von Haselberg
(edition of 6)

1258 BLUEBELL WOOD   *
audio visual
Sean Dower
(edition of 5)

1259 BEATING THE BRIDGES   *
audio visual
William Raban

1260 LET'S STAY WITH THESE PICTURES   *
audio visual
Terry Smith
(edition of 5)

1261 TEA LEAVES   NFS
audio visual
Matthew Grinter (Producer, Luke Thornton)

1262 STRIPS (VERTICAL)   NFS
audio visual
Matt Calderwood

1263 ETHEL AND THE MUTANT BABIES   *
audio visual
Vicky Hawkins
(edition of 25)

1264 FIVE DRAWINGS   NFS
audio visual
Anne Bean

1265 BODDINGTON: HIS THOUGHTS CAN KILL   *
audio visual
Guy Oliver
(edition of 10)

1266 TURNING THE PLACE OVER   *
audio visual
Richard Wilson RA
(edition of 5: £1,000 each)

* Refer to Sales Desk

LIST OF EXHIBITORS

Abegunde, Ademola, SABE, University of Westminster, 35 Marylebone Road, London NW1 5LS, **866**

Abel, Susan, 8 Meadhope Street, Wolsingham, Bishop Auckland, Durham DL13 3EN, **448**

Ablitt, Matthew, 5B Sharon Gardens, London E9 7RX, **192, 401**

ABRAHAMS, Prof. Ivor, RA, 18 Spezia Road, London NW10 4QJ, **956, 957, 958, 959, 960, 961**

ACKROYD, Prof. Norman, CBE RA, 1 Morocco Street, London SE1 3HB, **107, 112, 113, 114, 115, 116**

A'Court, Angela, 1460 Lexington Avenue, Apartment 1, New York, NY 10128, USA, **335**

Agis, Maurice, 6 Kirton Gardens, London E2 7LS, **985**

AITCHISON, Craigie, CBE RA, c/o Advanced Graphics London 32 Long Lane, London SE1 4AY, **99**

Al-Assadi, Selvei, Grove Dell, Pump Lane North, Marlow, Buckinghamshire SL7 3RD, **798**

Albrecht, Gretchen, c/o Flat 2, 104 Harmood Street, London NW1 8DS, **45**

Alcaman, Rocio, Mar Blanco 1842, Vitacura, Santiago 6680672, Chile, **415**

Alcock, Anna, Inky Cuttlefish Studios, Lower Ground Floor, 5 Blackhorse Lane, London E17 6DS, **428, 429**

Alex Flint and David Shanks, Flat 3, 17 Princes Avenue, Princes Park, Liverpool, Merseyside L8 2TB, **908**

Alexander, Naomi, 6 The Bishops Avenue, Finchley, London N2 0AN, **326, 436**

Allford Hall Monaghan Morris, 2nd Floor, Block C, Morelands, 5-23 Old Street, London EC1V 9HL, **844, 864**

ALSOP, Prof. William, OBE RA, Alsop Architects, Parkgate Studio, 41 Parkgate Road, London SW11 4NP, **754, 769, 770, 792, 849, 857**

ANDO, Tadao, Hon RA, Tadao Ando Architects and Associates, 5-23 Toyosaki 2-Chome, Kita-Ku Osaka, 531 0072, Japan, **786**

Andrews, Carole, Wychling House, Wichling, Sittingbourne, Kent ME9 0DP, **269**

Baker, Richard, 26 Aviary Place, Leeds, West Yorkshire
LS12 2NP, **339**

Balaam, Louise, 81 Brittains Lane, Sevenoaks, Kent
TN13 2JS, **342**

Baldwin, Janine, 19 Gladstone Road, Scarborough,
North Yorkshire YO12 7BQ, **759**

Baldwin, Warren, 2 Leaphill Road, Bournemouth,
Dorset BH7 6LU, **536**

BALMER, Derek, Hon Member Ex Officio PRWA,
c/o Royal West of England Academy, Queens Road,
Clifton, Bristol BS8 1PX, **1139**

Bandola, Margot, 2 Dundonald Road, Ramsgate, Kent
CT11 9TB, **479**

Banfield, Sarah, 143 Southampton Road, Northampton,
NN4 8DZ, **378**

Barber, George, 9 Roderick Road, London NW3 2NN, **1251**

Barnes, Jeanette, Flat 14, Old Park House, Old Park
Road, London N13 4RD, **753**

Bartlett, Adrian, 132 Kennington Park Road, London
SE11 4DJ, **377**

BASELITZ, Georg, Hon RA, Courtesy of the Artist +
Jay Jopling/White Cube, London, **8**

Battle, Jay, Hart Gallery, 113 Upper Street, London
N1 1QN, **766**

Battle, Sarah, 11 Harrop Green, Diggle, Oldham, Greater
Manchester OL3 5LW, **176**

Baumgartner, Christiane, Courtesy of Alan Cristea
Gallery, 31 Cork Street, London W1S 3NU, **90, 91**

Bauzys, Aurimas, SABE, University of Westminster,
35 Marylebone Road, London NW1 5LS, **793**

Baztan Rodriguez, Pedro, Flat 25, 50 Well Street, London
E9 7PX, **492, 545**

Bean, Anne, 80 Three Colt Street, London E14 8AP, **1264**

BEATTIE, Basil, RA, 1 The Village School House, Lower
Green West, Mitcham CR4 3AF, **38, 39**

Bedward, Matthew, bblur Architecture, 50 Shad
Thames, London SE1 2LY, **877**

Beeson, Peter, 12 Bellair Terrace, St Ives, Cornwall TR26 1JR, **713**

BELLANY, Dr John, CBE HRSA RA, c/o Beaux Arts (London), 22 Cork Street, London W1S 3NA, **1135, 1170, 1215, 1226, 1229**

Bellou, Rania, Flat 11, Greatorex House, Greatorex Street, London E1 5NS, **558, 559**

Ben Cowd and Tobias Klein, 17B Caversham Road, London NW5 2DT, **811**

Ben Langlands & Nikki Bell, Courtesy of Alan Cristea Gallery, 31 Cork Street, London W1S 3NU, **643**

BENSON, Prof. Gordon, OBE RA, Benson and Forsyth LLP, 37D Mildmay Grove North, London N1 4RH, **833, 834, 835, 836**

BERG, Adrian, RA, c/o Royal Academy of Arts, **937, 938, 950, 964, 965, 966**

BEVAN, Tony, RA, c/o Ben Brown Fine Arts, 21 Cork Street, London W1S 3LZ, **27, 28**

Birchall, Chrissie, 2 Coastguard Cottages, Lepe, Southampton, Hampshire SO45 1AD, **447**

Bird, Christie, Wellesley House, Blackbridge Road, Freshwater Bay, Isle of White PO40 9QP, **300**

Birds Portchmouth Russum Architects, Unit 11, Union Wharf, 23 Wenlock Road, London N1 7SB, **799, 846**

Birkett, Hannah, 75 Elderfield Road, London E5 0LE, **494, 1012**

Birtwhistle, Rosie, Woodvilla, Medway Drive, East Grinstead, West Sussex RH19 4NB, **298**

BLACKADDER, Dame Elizabeth, DBE RA, 57 Fountainhall Road, Edinburgh, EH9 2LH, **1120, 1144, 1180, 1188, 1234**

Blake, Adrienne, 6 Eden Road, Tunbridge Wells, Kent TN1 1TS, **749, 751**

Blees Luxemburg, Rut, Flat 72, Thaxted Court, London N1 7QQ, **13**

Bliss, Ian, 10 Vicarage Lane, Wing, Leighton Buzzard, Bedfordshire LU7 0NU, **553**

Bodiam, Michael, Unit 3D, West Wing Oslo House, 20 Felstead Street, London E9 5LT, **1056**

Borrington, David, 7 Lewis Lane, Arlesey, Bedfordshire SG15 6FB, **373**

Boshier, Derek, c/o Flowers, 82 Kingsland Road, London E2 8DP, **756, 758**

Boulting, Bridget, 84 Sarsfeld Road, London SW12 8HP, **738**

Bourgeois, Louise, Courtesy of Marlborough Fine Art, 6 Albemarle Street, London W1S 4BY, **262**

Bower, Susan, Larchfield House, Church Street, Barkston Ash, Tadcaster, North Yorkshire LS24 9PJ, **1187**

Bowers, Bernard, 42 Friern Road, London SE22 0AX, **1075**

Bowery, Dawn, 51 Grove Lane, Kingston upon Thames KT1 2SR, **1083**

BOWEY, Olwyn, RA, 4 Peace Road, Heyshott, Midhurst, West Sussex GU29 0DF, **297, 322, 1151**

Bowles, Sasha, 17 The Pleasance, London SW15 5HF, **1124, 1134**

BOWLING, Frank, OBE RA, c/o Rollo Contemporary Art, 51 Cleveland Street, London W1T 4JH, **617, 618, 619, 620, 621, 622**

Bowman, Edward, 4 Carlton Close, London NW3 7UA, **1046**

BOWYER, William, RA, 12 Cleveland Avenue, Chiswick, London W4 1SN, **117, 1095, 1116, 1132, 1211, 1212**

Bradford, Shane, 15 Tanner House, Tanner Street, London SE1 3LL, **646**

Braven, Angela, Harpsichord House, Cobourg Place, Hastings, East Sussex TN34 3HY, **473, 691**

Brayne, David, 4 Enfield Terrace, Weymouth Road, Evercreech, Somerset, BA4 6JE, **475, 529**

Brennan, Jessie, Flat 2, Hanson House, Pinchin Street, London E1 1PD, **52, 370**

Brodholt, Gail, Half Moon Studio, Unit F1, 245A Coldharbour Lane, London SW9 8RR, **249**

Brooking, Paul, The Old Wall, 6 Upper Butts, Brentford TW8 8DA, **1063**

BROWN, Ralph, RA, Southanger Farm, Chalford, Stroud, Gloucester, **1216, 1217, 1218, 1243, 1244, 1245**

Brujis, Julio, Flat 81, Matilda House, St Katharines Way, London E1W 1LG, **1031**

Brunner, Norbert, Gaudenz Dorfer Guertel 43-45/3A, Vienna A-1120, **859, 860**

Buchanan, Kyle, 50 Clarence Square, Cheltenham, Gloucestershire GL50 4JR, **903**

Buck, Jon, c/o Gallery Pangolin, Unit 9 Chalford Ind. Estate, Chalford, Gloucestershire GL6 8NT, **686**

Buckley, Patricia, 8 Kingfisher Lodge, Strawberry Vale, Twickenham TW1 4SL, **501**

Burnstone, Deborah, 25 Lucerne Road, London N5 1TZ, **711**

Burtynsky, Edward, c/o Flowers East, 82 Kingsland Road, London E2 8DP, **10, 1061**

BUTLER, James, MBE RA, Valley Farm Studios, Radway, Warwick, CV35 0UJ, **280, 438, 564, 565, 566**

Butterworth, John, 10 Railway Avenue, Whitstable, Kent CT5 1LJ, **329**

C

Calderwood, Matt, Studio 7, Chisenhale Studios, 64-84 Chisenhale Road, London E3 5QZ, **1250, 1262**

Calvocoressi, Natalia, 175 York Way, London N7 9LN, **1050, 1085**

CAMP, Jeffery, RA, c/o Art Space Gallery, 84 St Peter's Street, London N1 8JS, **580, 581, 582, 583, 584, 585**

Campion, John, 194 Owens Avenue, Mount Brown, Dublin 8, Ireland, **791**

Capper, James, 15-25 Howie Street, London SW11 4AS, **1088**

CARO, Sir Anthony, OM CBE RA, Barford Sculptures, 38C Georgiana Street, London NW1 0EB, **15, 19, 1020**

Carpanini, David L, Fernlea, 145 Rugby Road, Milverton, Leamington Spa, Warwickshire CV32 6DJ, **412, 1153**

Carreck, Louise, 8 Downsbridge Road, Beckenham, Kent BR3 5HX, **1029**

Carter, Andrew, 44 Landells Road, East Dulwich, London SE22 9PQ, **425, 381**

CARTER, John, RA, 71A Westbourne Park Road, London W2 5QH, **257, 259, 265, 266, 657**

Carter, Mary, 2 Hodges Cottages, Hemyock, Cullompton, Devon EX15 3RW, **1186**

Carter, Tony, 2 Little Brownings, London SE23 3XJ, **270**

Cembrowicz, Cordelia, 3 Elver Gardens, Bethnal Green, London E2 7AZ, **393**

CHAMBERS, Stephen, RA, c/o Royal Academy of Arts, **59, 71, 590, 591, 592, 593**

Champion, Rachael, 82 Lea Bridge Road, London E5 9QD, **124**

Charman, George, Flat 2, Hanson House, Pinchin Street, London E1 1PD, **222**

Chaudhuri, Nandita, 35 Queen's Gate Terrace, Kensington, London SW7 5PN, **712, 733**

Cheese, Chloe, 58 Hyndewood, Bampton Road, Forest Hill, London SE23 2BJ, **177**

Chillemi, Onofrio, 49 Fawcett Close, Battersea, London SW11 2LT, **789**

CHIPPERFIELD, Prof. David, CBE RA, David Chipperfield Architects, Cobham Mews, Agar Grove, London NW1 9SB, **922, 923, 924, 925, 926**

Chouhan, Anahita, SABE, University of Westminster, 35 Marylebone Road, London NW1 5LS, **861**

Chrisostomou, Petros, 25 Ashbourne Avenue, Whetstone, London N20 0AL, **1060**

CHRISTOPHER, Ann, RA, c/o Royal Academy of Arts, **651, 654, 674, 675, 676**

Chuang, Yaojen, Flat 30, McGlashon House, Hunton Street, London E1 5EZ, **886, 887**

Clark, Mary, 11 Tory, Bradford-on-Avon BA15 1NN, **198**

Clark, Rachel, 10 Denman Road, London SE15 5NP, **255**

CLARKE, Carey, Hon Member Ex Officio PPRHA, 16 Joyce Avenue, Foxrock, Dublin 18, Eire, **1145**

Coombes, Matthew, 54 Lawrence Road, London
N15 4EG, **67, 73**

Cooper, David, 23 Forest Glade, London E11 1LU, **290**

COOPER, Eileen, RA, c/o Art First Gallery, 9 Cork Street,
London W1S 3LL, **80, 88, 227, 228, 1129, 1130**

Coryndon, Sophie, 48 The Village, Alciston Village,
Polegate, East Sussex BN26 6UR, **287**

Coventry, Keith, 31 Museum Street, London WC1A 1LH,
141

Cox, Alan, 33 Charlotte Road, London EC2A 3PB, **69**

Cox, Martin, 7 Richmond Avenue, London N1 ONE, **336**

Coyne, Roderick, Bourne Cottage, Water End, Ashdon,
Saffron Walden, Essex CB10 2NA, **897, 898**

CRAIG-MARTIN, Michael, CBE RA, Courtesy of Gagosian
Gallery, 6–24 Britannia Street, London WC1X 9JD,
44, 637, Courtesy of Alan Cristea Gallery, 31 & 34 Cork
Street, London W1S 3NU **20, 638, 1022**

Crewe, Pamela, Becksbridge Studio, 113 Pelsall Road,
Brownhills, Walsall, WS8 7DL, **540**

Crittenden, James, 100 Alliance Road, London SE18 2AY,
526

Crook, P J, The Old Police Station, 39 Priory Lane,
Bishops Cleeve, Cheltenham, Gloucestershire
GL52 8JL, **1111**

Crosby, Dido, 52 Thorne Road, London SW8 2BY, **272**

Croucher, Cyril, 2 Bullock Market Terrace, Penzance,
Cornwall TR18 2PU, **1125**

CULLINAN, Edward, CBE RA, Edward Cullinan Architects,
1 Baldwin Terrace, London N1 7RU, **807, 885, 921**

CUMING, Frederick, RA, The Gables, Wittersham Road,
Iden, TN31 7UY, **119, 120, 1159, 1160, 1168, 1169**

Cummings, Novette, 16 Leysfield Road, London W12 9JF,
714

CUMMINS, Gus, RA, Harpsichord House, Cobourg Place,
Hastings, Sussex TN34 3HY, **600, 601, 975**

Curtis, Andrew, 7 Reventlow Road, London SE9 2DJ, **104**

Curtis, Ellie, 17 Sheridan House, Hawksley Road, London
N16 0TB, **416**

D

DANNATT, Prof. Trevor, RA, Dannatt, Johnson Architects, 52C Borough High Street, London SE1 1XN, **881, 882, 883**

Davenport, Ian, Courtesy of Alan Cristea Gallery, 31 Cork Street, London W1S 3NU, **206**

Davidge, Claire, 96 Crofton Road, London SE5 8NA, **506**

Davies, Mick, 171 Highbury Hill, London N5 1TB, **324**

Davis, Michael Robert, 8A Ebsworth Street, London SE23 1ES, **757**

de Bono, Michael, 11 Branwen Close, Culver House Cross, Cardiff CF5 4NE, **1149, 1164**

de Coo, Inez, 6 Raveley Street, London NW5 2HU, **1027**

DE GREY, Spencer, CBE RA, Foster + Partners, Riverside Three, 22 Hester Road, London SW11 4AN, **889, 930, 932,**

De Jong, Carole, 70 Clarence Way, London NW1 8DG, **413**

De Monchaux, Paul, 56 Manor Avenue, London SE4 1TE, **49**

Deadman, Jeremy, 62A Walden Avenue, Chislehurst, Kent BR7 6EW, **126**

Dean, John, Flat 1, 1 Elm Road, London SW14 7JL, **1021**

DEAN, Tacita, RA, Courtesy of the Artist, Frith Street Gallery and Marian Goodman Gallery, New York and Paris, **672**

Debenham, Charles, Little Simons, Oldhouse Road, Great Horkesley CO6 4EQ, **557**

Dennis, Jeffrey, c/o Michael Richardson Contemporary Art, 84 St Peter's Street, London N1 8JS, **144, 944**

Design Research Unit Wales, c/o Matthew Jones Welsh School Of Architecture, Bute Building, King Edward VII Avenue, Cardiff, Caerdydd CF10 3NB, **933**

Di Stefano, Arturo, c/o Purdy Hicks Gallery, 65 Hopton Street, London SE1 9GZ, **53**

DICKSON, Dr Jennifer, RA, 20 Osborne Street, Ottawa, Ontario K1S 4Z9, Canada, **244, 245, 258, 263, 264**

Dine, Jim, Courtesy of Alan Cristea Gallery, 31 Cork Street, London W1S 3NU, **163**

Dinnis, Richard, 1 Pendennis Rise, Falmouth, Cornwall TR11 4LT, **434**

Dodd, Ben, 23 Churchbury Road, Enfield EN1 3HR, **1253**

Dower, Sean, 387A Southwark Park Road, London SE16 2JH, **1248, 1258**

Downes, Willemien, Merrymead, Lime Grove, West Clandon, Surrey GU4 7UT, **343**

Doyle, Morgan, 55 Argyll Mansions, 303–323 Kings Road, London SW3 5ER, **971**

DRAPER, Kenneth, RA, Carrer Gran 55A,07720 Es Castell, Menorca, Spain, **678, 1014, 1015, 1016, 1017, 1018**

Drescher, Lauren, Flat 2, Royal Victoria Patriotic Building, London SW18 3SX, **422**

Duffin, John, 13 Marsala Road, London SE13 7AA, **426, 525**

Dunseath, Chris, The Priory, High Street, Hinton St George, Somerset TA17 8SE, **763, 767**

DUNSTAN, Bernard, RA PPRWA, 10 High Park Road, Kew, Richmond, Surrey TW9 4BH, **532, 535, 544, 548**

Durbar, Khadija, SABE, University of Westminster, 35 Marylebone Road, London NW1 5LS, **796**

DURRANT, Jennifer, RA, La Vigna, Via Bondi 14, 06069 Tuoro-Sul-Trasimeno (PG), Italy, **605, 606, 607, 608, 736, 737,**

Dutton, Meg, 19 Morella Road, London SW12 8UQ, **260**

Dyson, Anthony, 61 Hampton Road, Teddington TW11 0LA, **409**

Dyson, Chris, 11 Princelet Street, London E1 6QH, **878**

E

Easton, Bella, 40 Ruskin Walk, London SE24 9LZ, **427**

Eaves, Sylvia, 50 Belsize Park Gardens, London NW3 4ND, **376**

Eisa, Ali, 36 Homefield Road, London W4 2LW, **95**

Eldridge Smerin Architects, c/o Nick Eldridge, Eldridge Smerin, 17 Calico Row, Plantation Wharf, London SW11 3TW, **856**

Elezis, Konstantinos, 58A Cephas Avenue, London E1 4AR, **805**

Elliott Bates, Joan, 17 Marlow Mill, Mill Road, Marlow, Buckinghamshire, SL7 1QD, **541**

EMIN, Tracey, RA, Courtesy of the Artist, **136, 579**

Emsens, Benedicte, 21 Kildare Gardens, London W2 5JS, **152**

Emsley, Paul, c/o Redfern Gallery, 20 Cork Street, London W1X 1PF, **223**

Evans, Mark, 39 Gernons, Basildon, Essex SS16 5TN, **493**

EYTON, Anthony, RA, Courtesy of Browse and Darby, 19 Cork Street, London W1S 3LP, **1103, 1131, 1137, 1140, 1228, 1236**

F

Fairfax-Lucy, Edmund, Charlecote Park, Warwick CV35 9ER, **289**

Farago, Leslie, 109D Coningham Road, London W12 8BU, **346**

Farley, Lucy, 1 Belmont Court, Pembroke Mews, London W8 6ES, **203, 209**

Farman, John, Flat 7, Royal Victoria Patriotic Building, John Archer Way, London SW18 3SX, **439**

Farrell, Anthony, 6 Avenue Road, Leigh-on-Sea, Essex SS9 1AX, **394**

Farrer, Rosemary, Stoke Farmhouse, Beechingstoke, Pewsey, Wiltshire SN9 6HQ, **496**

FARTHING, Prof. Stephen, RA, 16 John Islip Street, London SW1P 4JU, **602, 603, 604, 1165**

Faulds, Gordon, Studio 22, Hamilton Road, Taunton TA1 2ER, **703**

Fawcett, David, 39 Dorking Road, Tunbridge Wells TN1 2LN, **503**

Fay, Helen, 41 Kitchener Terrace, North Shields, Tyne and Wear, NE30 2HH, **236**

FEDDEN, Mary, OBE RA PPRWA, c/o Royal Academy of Arts, **1141, 1142, 1143, 1148**

Feix&Merlin Architects, Unit 29, The Paragon, 43 Searles Road, London SE1 4YL, **794, 855**

Felts, Shirley, 4 Rocque Lane, London SE3 9JN, **306**

Fishpool, Megan, 57A Talfourd Road, London SE15 5NN, **183**

FLANAGAN, Barry, OBE RA, Courtesy of Waddington Galleries Ltd, 11 Cork Street, London W1S 3LT, **1246**

Flannigan, Moyna, 3/2 Logan Street, Edinburgh EH3 5EN, **93, 92**

Ford, Peter, 13 Cotswold Road, Windmill Hill, Bristol BS3 4NX, **408**

Foreman, Margaret, Flint House, 21 Harbour Street, Broadstairs, Kent CT10 1ET, **518**

Forsythe, Max, 1A The Terrace, Richmond Hill, Richmond TW10 6RN **1077**

Foster, Grant, Unit 2B Oslo House, West Wing, 20 Felstead Street, London E9 5LT, **327**

FOSTER OF THAMES BANK, Lord, OM RA, Foster + Partners, Riverside, 22 Hester Road, London SW11 4AN, **818, 847, 927**

Fountain, Marian, 8 Rue Des Prairies, Paris 75020, France, **781**

Fowler, Jaana, 42 Winton Avenue, London N11 2AT, **764**

Fox, Jo, 2 Old Park Cottages, Woodbury Lane, Nr Axminster, Devon EX13 5TL, **538**

Fox Ockinga, Marianne, 6 Thornhill Square, London N1 1BQ, **382**

Francis, Anthony, 69A Chatsworth Road, London E5 0LH, **1006**

FRASER, Donald Hamilton, RA, Braham Cottage, Remenham Lane, Remenham, Henley-on-Thames, Berkshire, RG9 2LR, **1179, 1227**, c/o CCA Galleries, The Studio, Greenhill Estate, Tilford Road, Tilford, Surrey GU10 2DY, **199, 241, 1213, 1214**

FREETH, Peter, RA, 83 Muswell Hill Road, London N10 3HT, **156, 239, 246, 247, 253, 396**

Friend and Company Architects, 31 Oval Road, London NW1 7EA, **888**

Fromm, Lilo, 7 Wesley Square, London W11 1TP, **420**

Frost, Anthony, c/o Advanced Graphics London, 32 Long Lane, London SE1 4AY, **168**

G

Gale, Colin, 161 Hollydale Road, London SE15 2TF, **165**

Gardiner, Anna, 59A Portobello Road, London W11 3DB, **397, 1123**

Gibbons, John, c/o Flowers East, 82 Kingsland Road, London E2 8DP, **984, 1087**

Gifford, Jane, 69 Finsbury Park Road, London N4 2JY, **561**

Gili, Katherine, 7 The Mall, Faversham, Kent ME13 8JL, **987**

Gillman, Tricia, 149 Algernon Road, London SE13 7AP, **967**

Gilmartin, Patrick, 2B Pilgrims Lane, London NW3 1SL, **747**

Girling, Sheila, 111 Frognal, Hampstead, London NW3 6XR, **998**

Glanville, Chris, Galveston, Giggs Hill Road, Thames Ditton, Surrey KT7 0BT, **527**

Goldberg, Anne, 16 Valley Road, Cheadle SK8 1HY, **539**

Golding, Gillian, 92 Manor Avenue, Brockley, London SE4 1TE, **142**

GORE, Frederick, CBE RA, Flat 3, 35 Elm Park Gardens, London SW10 9QF, **24, 1152, 1158, 1225, 1235, 1237**

GORMLEY, Antony, OBE RA, c/o Royal Academy of Arts, **661**

Gorresio, Livia Paola, 35 Cheryls Close, London SW6 2AY, **995**

GOUGH, Piers, CBE RA, CZWG Architects LLP, 17 Bowling Green Lane, London EC1R 0QB, **931**

Gracia, Carmen, 65 Westover Road, High Wycombe, Buckinghamshire HP13 5HX, **162**

Granger-Taylor, Nicolas, 11 Brierley Road, London SW12 9LY, **451**

GREEN, Anthony, RA, c/o Whitcombe Associates,
62 Cloncurry Street, London SW6 6DU, **51, 214, 1230,**
The Print Studio Cambridge Ltd, Building 10, Michael
Young Centre, Purbeck Road, Cambridge CB2 8HN,
213

Green, Matthew, 220C Stoke Newington High Street,
London N16 7HU, **363**

Griffiths, Peter, 21 Brown Street, Sheffield S1 2BS, **1011**

GRIMSHAW, Sir Nicholas, CBE PRA, Grimshaw,
57 Clerkenwell Road, London EC1M 5NG, **384, 406,
795, 839, 902**

Grinter, Matthew, 17 Victoria Road, Warmley, Bristol,
Gloucestershire BS30 5JZ, **1261**

Grover, Martin, Flat 2, 31 Morrish Road, Brixton, London
SW2 4EB, **507**

Gumuchdjian, Philip, 17 Rosebery Avenue, London
EC1R 4SP, **884**

Gustard, Tim, Silverdale, St John's Road, Stainton,
Penrith, Cumbria CA11 0EQ, **500**

Gutsche, Claas, Flat 15, Brocket House, Union Road,
London SW8 2RE, **184, 188**

Gutschow, Beate, Courtesy of Eric Frank Fine Art
London; Produzentengalerie, Hamburg; Sonnabend
Gallery, New York, **652, 653**

H HADID, Zaha, CBE RA, Studio 9, 10 Bowling Green Lane,
London EC1R 0BD, **824, 825, 826, 827, 867**

Hakamada, Hiroto, Salahoona, Spiddal, Co. Galway,
Ireland, **358**

Hall, Michael, 12 Caulfield Road, London SE15 2DE, **157,
387**

HALL, Nigel, RA, 11 Kensington Park Gardens, London
W11 3HD, **36, 40, 677**

Hall, Tim, 11A Cromwell Grove, London W6 7RQ, **1067**

Hamilton, Julia, 128 Middleton Road, London E8 4LP,
347, 739

Hamilton, Susie, 23 Rhondda Grove, London E3 5AP,
1004

Hammick, Tom, West Beam, Henley Down, Nr. Battle,
East Sussex TN33 9BN, **117**

Hampson, Mark, 17 Eastfield Road, London E17 3BA, **131**

Hanscomb, Brian, Tor View, Limehead, St Breward,
Bodmin, Cornwall PL30 4LU, **366**

Hanselaar, Marcelle, 58 Eccleston Square, London
SW1V 1PH, **182**

Hanson, Brian, 1 The Smithy, Wadhurst, East Sussex
TN5 6JQ, **323**

Hardy, Robert, 24 Albemarle Road, East Barnet,
Hertfordshire EN4 8EG, **293**

Hargreaves, Barton, Flat 2, 15 Goulton Road, Clapton,
London E5 8HA, **64, 1072**

Harnett, Marie, Courtesy of Alan Cristea Gallery, 31 Cork
Street, London W1S 3NU, **389, 424**

Harris, Jennifer, Berry House, Cheriton Fitzpaine,
Nr. Crediton, Devon EX17 4HZ, **455**

Harris, Roger, Springhill Cottage, Quarhouse,
Brimscombe, Stroud, Gloucestershire GL5 2RS, **193**

Harris, Mark, 14 Victoria Road, Kingston Upon Thames
KT1 3DW, **125, 189**

Harvey, Marcus, Courtesy of the Artist and Jay Jopling,
White Cube, London, **614, 689**

Hassim, Oona, 44 Richmond Avenue, London N1 0ND,
433

Hatfull, Nicholas, 109C Parnell Road, London E3 2RT, **197**

Havsteen-Franklin, Eleanor, 50 Marshall Avenue,
St Albans AL3 5HS, **180**

Hawdon, Paul, 62 Marshall Road, Cambridge CB1 7TY,
403

Hawkins, Vicky, Flat 82, Charles Dickens House, 130
Mansford Street, London E2 6LU, **1263**

Haxworth, Hetty, Tullo Farm, Menmuir, Edzell, Brechin,
Angus, Scotland DD9 7UH, **110**

Haydock-Wilson, Paul, 8 New Butt Lane, London
SE8 4SL, **1082**

Hayes, Jeannette, Studio 3E, Cooper House, 2 Michael
Road, London SW6 2AD, **364**

Hearle, Rebecca, 19 Station Road North, Walpole Cross
   Keys, King's Lynn, Norfolk PE34 4HB, **354**
Heat, Ann, Stumps Grove Farm, Whitehill Lane,
   Ockham, Woking, Surrey GU23 6PJ, **456**
Hebson, Nadia, 2 The College, Durham DH1 3EQ, **301, 1118**
Hegarty, David, 34 Crescent Way, London SW16 3AJ, **722**
Heider, Christine, 20 Wimpole Street, London W1G 8GF,
   725
Held, Julie, 48 Barrington Road, London N8 8QS, **969**
Hemsworth, Gerard, 2A Tavistock Terrace, London
   N19 4DB, **968**
Henderson, Bill, 5 Rosendale Road, London SE21 8DS,
   705, 942
Hepburn, Fiona, 89 Park Avenue South, London
   N8 8LX, **221**
Herczeg, Joschi, 112B Evering Road, Stoke Newington,
   London N16 7BD, **1037**
Hewitt, John, 11 Harrop Green, Diggle, Saddleworth
   OL3 5LW, **224, 229**
Hicks, Nicola, Flowers East, 82 Kingsland Road, London
   E2 8DP, **983**
Hills, Alexander, The Old Rectory, Tittleshall, Norfolk
   PE32 2PN, **928**
Himsworth, Rhys, 147 Tower Gardens Road, London
   N17 7PE, **1065, 1066**
Hipkiss, Christine, Flat 24, Ashby Grange, Stafford Road,
   Wallington, Surrey SM6 9BE, **452**
Hirst, Damien, Collection of the Artist, **1247**
Hobson, Ann, Flat 1, 20 Allfarthing Lane, Wandsworth,
   London SW18 2PQ, **153**
Hogan, Eileen, 13 Wythburn Place, London W1H 7BU,
   465, 1138
Holden, John, 61 High Street, Long Buckby,
   Northamptonshire NN6 7RE, **1008**
Holder, Guy, 56 Addison Road, Hove, East Sussex
   BN3 1TP, **1089**
Holland, Charles, FAT, Unit 2, 49–59 Old Street, London
   EC1V 9HX, **868, 858**

Hopkins, Clyde, c/o Advanced Graphics London, 32 Long Lane, London SE1 4AY, **169, 976**

HOPKINS, Sir Michael, CBE RA, Hopkins Architects, 27 Broadley Terrace, London NW1 6LG, **904**

Horack-Elyafi, Hana, 2 Grassway, Wallington SM6 8DG, **704**

Howard, James, c/o Royal Academy of Arts, **1028**

HOWARD, Prof. Ken, RA, c/o Richard Green Gallery, 147 New Bond Street, London W1S 2TS, **1099, 1100, 1115, 1136, 1174, 1194**

Howorth, Diana, 1 Aspley Road, London SW18 2DB, **423**

HOYLAND, Prof. John, RA, c/o Royal Academy of Arts, **9, 1003, 43**

Hozic, Dzenana, Basement Flat, 16A Wren Street, London WC1X 0HB, **1047**

Hubbard, Samuel, Ground Floor Flat, 8 Marlborough Road, Falmouth, Cornwall TR11 3LP, **399**

Humphreys, David, Maudlin Hill House, Sopers Lane, Steyning, West Sussex BN44 3PU, **515**

Humphreys, Ian, Heir Island, Skibbereen, Co. Cork, Republic of Ireland, **699**

Humphreys, John, Beach Crest, Normans Bay, Pevensey, East Sussex BN24 6PS, **271**

Hunt, Peter R, 5 Ripley View, Loughton, Essex IG10 2PB, **470**

Huson, Cedric, Sunnyside Croft, Overbrae, Nr. Turriff, Aberdeenshire AB53 5SL, **477, 554**

Hutchinson, Richard, 432B Kings Road, London SW10 0LJ, **400**

HUXLEY, Prof. Paul, RA, 2 Dalling Road, London W6 0JB, **41, 42**

I

Ian Simpson Architects, Riverside, 4 Commercial Street, Manchester M15 4RQ, **814**

Illum, Marina, 62 East Avenue, Oxford, Oxfordshire OX4 1XP, **853**

Imms, David, 6 Church Street, Finedon, Northamptonshire NN9 5NA, **1112**

Inshaw, David, 23 High Street, Devizes, Wiltshire
SN10 1AT, **1133**

IRVIN, Albert, RA, c/o Gimpel Fils, 30 Davies Street,
London W1K 4NB, **35, 639, 640, 641**, c/o Advanced
Graphics, 32 Long Lane, London SE1 4AY, **218, 219**

IRWIN, Flavia, RA, 5 & 6 Camer Street, Meopham, Kent
DA13 0XR, **14, 962, 963, 1232**

Isgar, Caroline, 6 Friendly Street, Deptford, London
SE8 4DT, **171, 202**

J

JACKLIN, Bill, RA, Courtesy of Marlborough Fine Art,
6 Albemarle Street, London W1S 4BY, **4, 200, 207,
252, 1108, 1109**

Jackson, Bridget H, 11 Parliament Court, Parliament Hill,
London NW3 2TS, **728**

Jackson, Dilys, 24 Llanedeyrn Road, Penylan, Cardiff,
Caerdydd CF23 9DX, **782**

Jackson, Vanessa, 169 Bermondsey Street, London
SE1 3UW, **57, 58**

Jadric, Mladen, Mladen Jadric Architects,
Kalvarienberggasse 74, 1170 Wien, Austria, **840, 841**

James, Jeffrey, 11 Atlas Mews, Ramsgate Street, London
E8 2NE, **843**

Jampel, Aileen, 19 Edmunds Walk, London N2 0HU, **385**

Jaray, Tess, 29 Camden Square, London NW1 9XA, **47**

Jewell, Dick, H Block, Flat 5, Peabody Avenue, London
SW1V 4AT, **127, 137**

JIRICNA, Eva, CBE RA, Eva Jiricna Architects Ltd, Third
Floor, 38 Warren Street, London W1T 6AE, **812, 915,
916**

Joc, Jon & Josch, Flat 9, Metro Building, 200 Chandos
Road, London E15 1TB, **1069**

Johnson, Jeni, 18 Taylors Lane, Sydenham, London
SE26 6QL, **727**

Johnson, Michael, 15 Elsing Drive, King's Lynn, Norfolk
PE30 3UT, **450**

Johnson, Orlando, The Presidents Lodge, Wolfson
College, Cambridge CB3 9BB, **132**

Jonathan Gales & Claire Pepper, 109D Stamford Street, London SE1 9NN, **1030**

Jones, Neal, 32B Elder Avenue, London N8 8PS, **940, 941**

JONES, Allen, RA, Courtesy of Alan Cristea Gallery, 31 Cork Street, London W1S 3NU, **205**, c/o Royal Academy of Arts, **23, 25, 26, 273, 687**

Judge–Fürstova, Mila, RWA, Cheltenham Ladies College, Bayshill Road, Cheltenham GL50 3EP, **237, 238**

K

Kander, Nadav, c/o Flowers East, 82 Kingsland Road, London E2 8DP, **1079**

Kang, Eemyun, 13 St Leonards Mews, 251 Hoxton Street, London N1 5LG, **201, 208**

Karas, Vanja, 144 Holland Road, London W14 8BE, **1081**

Karnachev, Vladimir, c/o I.A.Iwegbu, 30 Pamela Road, Northfield, Birmingham B31 2QG, **513**

Kelly, Roger, 47 Printers Mews, London E3 5NZ, **138**

Kelly, Peter, The Chestnuts, The Square, Stock, Essex CM4 9LH, **321, 523**

Kennedy, Michael, 107 Knights Croft, New Ash Green, Longfield, Kent DA3 8HY, **284, 285**

Kenworthy–Browne, Fru, 6 Wray Crescent, London N4 3LP, **145**

Khan, Idris, Courtesy of Alan Cristea Gallery, 31 Cork Street, London W1S 3NU, **68**

KIDNER, Michael, RA, c/o Flowers East, 82 Kingsland Road, London E2 8DP, **567, 609, 610, 611, 612**

KIEFER, Anselm, Hon RA, Courtesy of the Artist and Jay Jopling/White Cube, London, **6**

Kihara, Yoshimi, 18 Woodriffe Road, London E11 1AH, **680, 982**

Kim, Hayoung, Royal Academy Schools, Burlington House, Piccadilly, London W1J 0BD, **234, 235**

KING, Prof. Phillip, CBE PPRA, 26 Savernake Road, London NW3 2JP, **632, 633, 634, 635, 636**

Kirkbride, Michael, 62 Hatley Close, London N11 3LN, **1104, 1110**

Kirwan, Richard, 72 Sandmere Road, Clapham, London SW4 7QH, **217**

Klein, Randy, 30 Homeleigh Road, London SE15 3EE, **981**

Klein, Tobias, 9 Wilmot Place, London NW1 9JP, **901**

KNEALE, Prof. Bryan, RA, courtesy of Cass Sculpture Foundation (www.sculpture.org.uk), **1**, 10A Muswell Road, Muswell Hill, London N10 2BG, **102, 648, 681, 683, 684**

Knell, Alex, 71 Thornton Avenue, Ground Floor Flat, London W4 1QF, **220, 1074**

Kolakowski, Matthew, 166 Brixton Road, London SW9 6AU, **337, 750**

KORALEK, Paul, CBE RA, Ahrends Burton and Koralek Architects, Studio 1, 7 Chalcot Road, London NW1 8LH, **785, 892, 893**

Kundi, Suzann, 61 Hampton Road, London E7 0NX, **230**

L

Lake, Alana, 75 Elderfield Road, London E5 0LE, **1051**

LANDY, Michael, RA, c/o Thomas Dane Gallery, 11 Duke Street, London SW1Y 6BN, **96, 215, 232, 233, 576, 577**

Lang, Liane, 15 Cornwall Crescent, London W11 1PH, **1078**

Lautman, Basia, Flat 16, 65 Finbrough Road, London SW10 9DW, **191**

Lawrence, John, 75 Elderfield Road, Hackney, London E5 0LE, **1024**

Lawrence, Peter, 48 Lonsdale Road, Oxford, Oxfordshire OX2 7EP, **158**

Lawson, Simon, Flat 1, 20 Allfarthing Lane, London SW18 2PQ, **100, 161**

LAWSON, Sonia, RA, c/o Royal Academy of Arts, **952, 953, 954, 1161, 1163, 1183**

Layzell, Peter, 72 Vale Road, Lancaster LA1 2JL, **305, 1178**

LE BRUN, Christopher, RA, c/o Royal Academy of Arts, **1202, 1203, 1204, 1205, 1206, 1233**

Leahy-Clark, Sharon, 187 Wellington Buildings, Ebury Bridge Road, London SW1W 8RX, **349**

Lush, Julie, 5 Providence Lane, Corsham, Wiltshire
SN13 9DJ, **449**

Lydbury, Jane, 101 Humber Road, London SE3 7LW,
365

Lynch, Patrick, 1 Amwell Street, London EC1R 1UL, **905**

M

Macalpine, Jean, Carrer Gran 55A, 07720 Es Castell,
Menorca, Spain, **155, 1055**

MACCORMAC, Sir Richard, CBE PPRIBA RA, MJP Architects,
9 Heneage Street, London E1 5LJ, **909, 920**

MACH, David, RA, 8 Havelock Walk, Forest Hill, London
SE23 3HG, **1041, 1193, 1210, 1239**

Mackechnie, John, 6 Holyrood Crescent, Glasgow
G20 6HJ, **60, 105**

Madden, David, 5 Dunbar Road, New Malden KT3 3RF,
462

Madgwick, Lee, 7 Queensway, King's Lynn, Norfolk
PE30 4AQ, **288, 516**

MAINE, John, RA, The Former School, East Knoyle,
Salisbury, Wiltshire SP3 6AF, **1201**

Major, Julie, 14 Onslow Gardens, London N10 3JU, **748,
779**

Malenoir, Mary, Tilford Green Cottage, Tilford, Farnham,
Surrey GU10 2BU, **708**

Mallows, Muriel, 10 Blandford Avenue, Oxford OX2 8DY,
499

MANASSEH, Leonard, OBE RA PPRWA, 6 Bacon's Lane,
Highgate Village, London N6 6BL, **275, 276, 277, 278,
279, 531**

MANSER, Michael, CBE RA, The Manser Practice, Bridge
Studios, 107A Hammersmith Bridge Road, London
W6 9DA, **895, 917**

Marbach, Emily Alexandra, 1 Kildare Terrace, London
W2 5JT, **283, 437**

March, Carl, 2 Lapworth Close, Greenlands, Redditch,
Worcestershire B98 7RJ, **392**

Marchant, David Edwin, 128 Overland Road, Mumbles,
Swansea, Abertawe SA3 4EU, **1092**

McNicol, Ian Cameron, 10 Carrick Road, Ayr, South
    Ayrshire KA7 2RB, **216**

McRae, Jennifer, Garden Flat, 3 Spencer Belle Vue, Bath,
    Somerset BA1 5ER, **1156, 1173**

Meazza, Luciana, Via Ausonio 7, 20123 Milano, Italy, **735,
945**

Medcalf, Gina, 64 Acre Lane, London SW2 5SP, **1010**

Melbourne, Dean, 58 Mount Road, Wordsley,
    Stourbridge, West Midlands DY8 5AR, **195**

Messenger, Sam, 72 Friern Road, London SE22 0AX, **160**

Messer, Peter, 5 Market Lane, Lewes, East Sussex
    BN7 2NT, **1147, 1150**

Metropolitan Workshop, 26 Oakford Road, London
    NW5 1AH, **773**

Michell, Patrick, Platform 5 Architects, Unit 1, 33
    Waterson Street, London E2 8HT, **828**

Middleton, Nicholas, 53 Montague Road, London
    E8 2HN, **395**

Midgley, Julia, The Hollies, 79 School Lane, Hartford,
    Cheshire CW8 1PG, **741**

Miers, Christopher, 114 Bishops Mansions, Bishops Park
    Road, London SW6 6DY, **318**

Miles, John, Sunnyside, Loders, Bridport, Dorset
    DT6 4NW, **185, 361**

Millar, Sandra, 64 Wood Vale, London SE23 3ED, **344,
368**

Miller, Andrew, 162 Church Road, London N17 8AS, **388,
390**

Miller, Melanie, 61 Connaught Road, Teddington,
    Middlesex TW11 0QF, **695**

Milo-Gray, Marcelle, Garden Cottage, North Street,
    Denbury, Devon TQ12 6DJ, **320, 546**

MILROY, Lisa, RA, Courtesy of Alan Cristea Gallery, 31 & 34
    Cork Street, London W1S 3NU, **623, 624**

Mitzman, Richard, Unit 1 Primrose Mews, Sharpleshall
    Street, London NW1 8YW, **803**

Mobbs, Nicholas, 371 Queens Road West, Beeston,
    Nottingham NG9 1GX, **251**

Monk, Simon, 26 Colchester Road, Southend-on-Sea, Essex SS2 6HP, **505**

MOON, Mick, RA, Courtesy of Alan Cristea Gallery, 31 Cork Street, London W1S 3NU, **662**

Morey de Morand, C, 61D Oxford Gardens, London W10 5UJ, **578, 946**

Morley, John, North Green Only, Stoven, Beccles NR34 8DE, **304**

Morris, Frederic, Flat 1, Belmont Court, Pembroke Mews, London W8 6ES, **240, 404**

Morris, Mali, 76 Royal Hill, London SE10 8RT, **30, 34**

Mortimer, Carey, Corso Vittorio Emanuele, 7, Bosa, Sardegna, 08013, Italy, **710**

Moss, Zoë, 12A Hervey Close, Finchley, London N3 2HD, **348**

Mounsey, Matthew, 16 White Cliff House, Vermont Road, London SW18 2LH, **701**

Moxhay, Suzanne, Flat 4, 38 Mount Ephraim Road, London SW16 1LW, **254, 1084**

Murray, Gail, 29 Kilgraston Road, Bridge of Weir, Renfrewshire PA11 3EN, **542**

Myerscough, Ishbel, 73 Colebrooke Row, London N1 8AA **359, 1114**

N

Narita, Miyako, 18B Ashby Street, London EC1V 0ED, **1039, 1252**

NASH, David, OBE RA, Capel Rhiw, Blaenau Ffestiniog, Gwynedd, North Wales LL41 3NT, **655**

Nathan, Janet, 19 Belsize Square, London NW3 4HT, **994**

Neal, Arthur, 32 Duke Street, Deal, Kent CT14 6DT, **709, 723**

Nevay, Heather, Courtesy of Portal Gallery, 15 New Cavendish Street, London W1G 9UB, **351**

New, Terry, 74 Florence Road, New Cross, London SE14 6QL, **986, 1035**

Newland, Paul, 14 Garden Street, Lewes, East Sussex BN7 1TJ, **740**

Nias, Samuel Luke, Flat 7, 23–25 Wilton Way, London
E8 3EE, **134**

Nicholson, Alison, Kennetts Cottage, Wittersham Road,
Peasmarsh, East Sussex TN31 6TD, **549**

Nurdan, Iskender, 27 Grafton Square, London SW4 0DB,
726

O

OCEAN, Humphrey, RA, 22 Marmora Road, London
SE22 0RX, **568, 569, 570, 571, 572, 573**

O'Connell, Eilis, The Creamery, Coolyduff, Inniscarra,
Co. Cork, Ireland, **685, 688**

O'Farrell, Liam, 139 Hassett Road, London E9 5SL, **483**

O'Keefe, Kevin, 40 Osborne Road, Southville, Bristol
BS3 1PW, **970**

Okubo, Sumiko, Takagi 3–361–15, Higashi Yamoto-shi,
Tokyo 207 0005, Japan, **154**

Oliver, Guy, 36 Barnet Gate Lane, Barnet EN5 2AB, **1265**

Oliver, Jason, 28 Longshore, London SE8 3DF, **149,
150**

Oloya, Peter, Gallery Pangolin, Unit 9 Chalford Industrial
Estate, Chalford, Gloucestershire GL6 8NT, **673**

Olrik, Trine, 52 Mildmay Road, London N1 4NG, **900**

O'Neill, Nigel, 20 Chancery House, Lowood Street,
London E1 0BU, **744, 989**

Onitolo, Abdul Hakim, Flat 69, Wayland House, Robsart
Street, London SW9 0BS, **1025**

Opie, Julian, Courtesy of Alan Cristea Gallery, 31 Cork
Street, London W1S 3NU, **1073**

Orchard, Elizabeth, 1 Sole Cottage, High Street,
Barcombe, East Sussex BN8 5BD, **314**

O'Reilly, Lesley, Flat 13, Elizabeth Blount Court,
48 Repton Street, London E14 7PZ, **435**

O'Reilly, Oran, Flat 13, Elizabeth Blount Court, 48 Repton
Street, London E14 7PZ, **129, 130**

ORR, Prof. Chris, MBE RA, 5 Anhalt Road, London
SW11 4NZ, **83, 84, 86, 87, 101, 1171**

Orrell, Jeanette, Trem Afon, Betws Gwerful Goch,
Corwen, Denbighshire LL21 9PT, **226**

P

Patel, Brijesh, 46 Liberty Street, London SW9 0EF, **1086**

Paterson, Isabel, 17 Chatsworth Avenue, London SW20 8JZ, **315**

Paul, Celia, Courtesy of Marlborough Fine Art, 6 Albemarle Street, London W1S 4BY, **123, 398**

Paul, Sylvia, 21 Empire Road, Harwich, Essex CO12 3QA, **721**

Payne, David, 25 Willmers Close, Bedford MK41 8DX, **308, 446**

Payne, Freya, c/o Flowers East, Flowers East, 82 Kingsland Road, London E2 8DP, **181**

Paynter, Hilary, Brunswick House, Torridge Hill, Bideford, Devon EX39 2AZ, **151**

Peace, John, 5 Loraine Terrace, Newcastle upon Tyne, Tyne and Wear NE15 8EA, **443**

Pearce, Theon, Basement Flat, 10A The Mount, St Leonards-on-Sea, East Sussex TN38 0HR, **353**

Pearman, Edd, Unit 47, Omega Works, 4 Roach Road, London E3 2PD, **174, 371**

Pearson, Andrew, 2 Ridgeway Cottages, Swanbourne, Milton Keynes MK17 0SJ, **550**

Perry, Peter, Stile Cottage, Trevithal, Paul, Penzance, Cornwall TR19 6UQ, **463**

Peter Barber Architects, 173 King's Cross Road, London WC1X 9BZ, **910**

Petterson, Melvyn, 47 Kinsale Road, London SE15 4HJ, **248**

Philippa Downes, Sarah Milburn, Julio Alves and Louise Fricker, Wellingtonia House, Tiddington Road, Stratford-upon-Avon, Warwickshire CV37 7AF, **934**

PHILLIPS, Tom, CBE RA, 57 Talfourd Road, London SE15 5NN, **50, 121, 122, 1231**

Phippen, Kerry, 146 Arrowsmith Drive, Stonehouse, Gloucestershire GL10 2QR, **345, 716**

Phipps, Howard, Hilfield, Homington Road, Coombe Bissett, Salisbury, Wiltshire SP5 4ND, **410**

Reeves, Philip, 13 Hamilton Drive, Hillhead, Glasgow
G12 8DN, **702**

Rego, Paula, Courtesy of Marlborough Fine Art Gallery,
6 Albemarle Street, London W1S 4BY, **77, 78**

Reid, Michael, 82 Albemarle Road, Beckenham
BR3 5HT, **402**

REMFRY, David, MBE RA, 19 Palace Gate, London W8 5LS,
1106, 1107, 1162, 1172

Resteghini, Giulia, Rothley Garden House,
Longwitton, Morpeth, Northumberland NE61 4JT,
225

Rey, Sandrine, 5 Allee du Bois Monsieur, Nozay 91620,
France, **562**

Rhys James, Shani, Dolypebyll, Llangadfan, Powys
SY21 0PU, **1101**

Richardson, Barbara, 71 Engadine Street, London
SW18 5BZ, **458**

Ridgwell, Martin, 14 Wanless Road, Herne Hill, London
SE24 0HW, **243**

Riley, Catherine, Lyndhurst, Midgley Road, Hebden
Bridge, West Yorkshire HX7 5LW, **405**

RITCHIE, Prof. Ian, CBE RA, c/o Ian Ritchie Architects,
110 Three Colt Street, London E14 8AZ, **852, 871, 872,
873, 874, 875**

Rivas Adrover, Esther, Flat 3, 53 Anson Road, London
NW2 3UY, **778**

Roantree, Christopher, 443 Kingsland Road, London
E8 4AU, **62**

Roberts, Simon, 26 Montgomery Street, Hove, East
Sussex BN3 5BF, **1049, 1062**

Robertson, Carol, Flowers East, 82 Kingsland Road,
London E2 8DP, **999, 1002**

Robertson, James Downie, RSA, Carruthmuir, by
Kilbarchan, Renfrewshire PA10 2QA, **1013**

Robin, Antoine, 21 Heaven Tree Close, London N1 2PW,
524

Robinson, Wayne, 254 Dentons Green Lane, Dentons
Green, St Helens, Merseyside WA10 6RY, **369, 417**

Rogers, Sarah, Knockarigg Cottage, Knockarigg, Grange
Pon, Wicklow, Ireland, **311**

ROGERS OF RIVERSIDE, Lord, CH RA, Rogers Stirk Harbour
+ Partners, Thames Wharf Studios, Rainville Road,
London W6 9HA, **808, 809, 914, 918, 919**

Rolfe, Nigel, 45 Inchicore Road, Dublin D8, Ireland, **1071**

Rolph, Danny, Courtesy of AR/Contemporary, Via
Vespucci 5, 20124 Milano, Italy, **690**

ROONEY, Mick, RA, 1 Sandford Rise, Charlbury, Chipping
Norton, Oxfordshire OX7 3SZ, **407**, c/o The Fosse
Gallery, The Square, Stow On The Wold, Cheltenham,
Gloucestershire GL54 1AF, **309, 1184, 1189, 1190, 1191**

Rose, Stephen, 26 Burnhill Road, Beckenham, Kent
BR3 3LA, **441**

Rosenthal, Steve, 7 A–Z studios, 3–5 Hardwidge Street,
London SE1 3SY, **1076**

ROSOMAN, Leonard, OBE RA, c/o The Fine Art Society,
148 New Bond Street, London W1S 2JT, **1105, 1207,
1208, 1209, 1240, 1241**

Ross, James, Waddington Galleries, Flat 2, 104 Harmood
Street, London NW1 8DS, **46**

Ross, John, Gloom Hall, 44 Beaumont Park Road,
Huddersfield, West Yorkshire HD4 5JS, **418**

Routh, Brian, 25 Ferens Haven, Holderness Road, Hull
HU8 9AH, **1249**

Rowbottom, Georgina, 212 Stony Lane, Burton,
Christchurch, Dorset BH23 7LB, **552**

Rowlett, George, c/o Art Space Gallery, 84 St Peter's
Street, London N1 8JS, **698, 996**

Royle, David, Courtesy of Beardsmore Gallery, 22 Prince
Of Wales Road, London NW5 3LG, **734, 742**

RUSCHA, Ed, Hon RA, Courtesy of the Artist and Gagosian
Gallery, **21**

Rushton, James, 17 Gower Street, Newcastle-under-
Lyme, Staffordshire ST5 1JQ, **312**

Rylands, Alison, 45 Garden Avenue, Mitcham, Surrey
CR4 2EE, **517**

Salmon, Christopher, 45 Rainbow Street, London
SE5 7TB, **421**

Salter, Anthony, 34 Lizban Street, Blackheath, London
SE3 8SS, **432**

Samways, Amelia, SABE, University of Westminster,
35 Marylebone Road, London NW1 5LS, **813**

SANDLE, Prof. Michael, RA, c/o Royal Academy of Arts, **1200**

Sandys, Timothy, Bankside Cottage, Petworth Road,
Witley, Surrey GU8 5PH, **679**

Sanei Hopkins Architects, 300 Aberdeen House, 22–24
Highbury Grove, London N5 2EA, **801, 850**

Sant, Mat, 93 Third Avenue, London W10 4HS, **61**

Sargent, Guy, Flat 3, Kara Lodge, 14 Newton Grove,
London W4 1LB, **1040**

Saull, Martin, 31 Tollgate Avenue, Redhill, Surrey
RH1 5HR, **362, 367**

Savva, Savva, c/o First Floor Flat (Rear), 22 Donovan
Avenue, London N10 2JX, **488**

Schmidt, Helga, Flat 5, 78 Cecile Park, London N8 9AU,
743

Schneider, Joseph, The Glass Door Unit 2–4, 10 Manor
Road, London N16 5SA, **350, 360**

SCOTT, Bill, Hon Member Ex Officio PRSA, 45 St Clair
Crescent, Roslin, Midlothian EH25 9NG, **771**

Scott, Inge Borg, Claymore House, Village Road,
Coleshill, Amersham, Buckinghamshire HP7 0LQ, **74**

Scrivener, Tony, Crandel, 28 Beaufoys Avenue,
Ferndown, Dorset BH22 9RH, **440, 478**

Sear, Helen, 3 High Street, Raglan, VSK, Gwent,
NP15 2DY, **1032**

Seeley, Eric, 4 Irwin Road, Bedford, MK40 3UL, **1197**

Selby, Richard, c/o Redfern Gallery, 20 Cork Street,
London W1X 1PF, **454**

Sepple, Rosa, 33 Hacton Lane, Hornchurch, Essex
RM12 6PH, **453**

Setch, Terry, c/o Art Space Gallery, 84 St Peter's Street,
London N1 8JS, **37**

Shafiei, Sara, Flat 2, 326 Finchley Road, London
 NW3 7AG, **775, 845**

Sheppard, Maurice, 33 St Martins Park, Crowhill,
 Haverfordwest, Pembrokeshire, SA61 2HP, **480**, **1195**

Shiomi, Nana, 96A Greenvale Road, London SE9 1PF,
 54, 56

Silverton, Norma, Apt. 11, 44 The Bishops Avenue,
 London N2 0BA, **170**

Sims, Ron, Bugle Cottage, 123 Tilkey Road, Coggeshall,
 Essex CO6 1QN, **521**

Sinkler, Paige, 18 Litchfield Way, Guildford, Surrey
 GU2 7QH, **1053**

Sixteen* (Makers), 22 Gordon Street, London WC1H 0QB,
 837

Skelcher, George, 7 Prideaux Place, Friars Place Lane,
 London W3 7AS, **332**

Sleigh, Bronwen, 58D Ferme Park Road, London
 N4 4ED, **143, 148**

Sloan, Joseph, Flat 11, Knightshayes House, 95 Holders
 Hill Road, London NW4 1JY, **374**

Small, David, Flat 55, Graham Mansions, Sylvester
 Road, London E8 1EU, **1000**

Smart, Robin, 16 Steeple Court, Coventry Road, London
 E1 5QZ, **386**

Smith, Alan, 32 Cleveland Park Avenue, London E17 7BS,
 147, 431

Smith,Bridget, Courtesy of the artist and Frith Street
 Gallery, London, **1026, 1080**

Smith, Donald, 52 The Green, Dartford, Kent DA2 6JT,
 777

Smith, Hazel, Mouse House, Hill Close, Reeth,
 Richmond, North Yorkshire DL11 6RX, **286**

Smith, Jenny, 29/8 Bellevue Road, Edinburgh,
 Midlothian, EH7 4DL, **694**

Smith, John, Tanya Leighton Gallery, Kurfürstenstraße
 156, 10785 Berlin, Germany **1254**

Smith, Richard, c/o Flowers East, 82 Kingsland Road,
 London E2 8DP, **575**

Smith, Terry, 19 Arrow Road, London E3 3HE, **1260**

Smith, Wendy, 2 Little Brownings, London SE23 3XJ,
664, 665

Smith Polyblank, Emily, Old Church School, The Street,
Shadoxhurst, Ashford, Kent TN26 1LU, **212**

Snelling, David, 15 Irene Road, London SW6 4AL, **328**

Songhurst, Anne, 7 Stotfold Road, Hitchin, Hertfordshire
SG4 0QN, **464**

Sorrell, Richard, Spindlewood, 50 High Street, Kintbury,
Hungerford, Berkshire RG17 9TN, **292, 303**

Spare, Richard, 72 Ravensbourne Park, London SE6 4XZ,
414, 118

Spee, Irene, Overschiese Dorpsstraat 43, Rotterdam,
3043 CN, Holland, **692**

Stallwood, Jane, 5 Middle Farm, Stainton, Barnard
Castle, Durham DL12 8RH, **514**

Stanley, Paula, 38 Portland Road, Bishop's Stortford,
Hertfordshire CM23 3SJ, **1009**

STELLA, Frank, Hon RA, Courtesy of Peter Freeman Inc.,
New York, **5, 7**

Stephenson Bell Architects, Aero Works, 5 Adair Street,
Manchester M1 2NQ, **822, 869**

Stibbon, Emma, c/o Upstairs Berlin, 133 Cumberland
Road, Bristol, Somerset BS1 6UX, **474**

Stieger, Jacqueline, Melton Hill Farm, South Lawn Way,
Melton, North Ferriby, East Riding of Yorkshire
HU14 3BL, **788**

Stjernsward, Philippa, 181B Lavender Hill, London
SW11 5TE, **31, 33**

Stocker, Geoffrey, 24 Centurion Rise, Hastings, East
Sussex TN34 2UL, **1052**

Stockham, Alfred, 75 Woodhill Road, Portishead,
Bristol, North Somerset BS20 7HA, **1196, 1198**

Stockwell, Hylton, Hoath Farm Cottage,
Mountfield, Robertsbridge, East Sussex TN32 5LJ,
274

Stoeger, Bernhard, Ligsalzstrasse 11, Munich 80339,
Germany, **783**

Stone, Adam, 10 Cookridge Drive, Leeds, West Yorkshire LS16 7LT, **341**

Stubbs, David, 133 Latimer Road, Eastbourne, East Sussex BN22 7JB, **487**

Studio Weave, Unit G1, Olympic House, 12 Somerford Grove, London N16 7RZ, **815, 819**

Sutton, Linda, 192 Battersea Bridge Road, London SW11 3AE, **310, 1199**

SUTTON, Philip, RA, 3 Morfa Terrace, Manorbier, Tenby, SA70 7TH, **627, 628, 629, 630, 631, 1102**

Sutton, Trevor, c/o Flowers East, 82 Kingsland Road, London E2 8DP, **717, 997**

Syed, Farah, 131B Leighton Road, London NW5 2RB, **72**

T

Taber, A Lincoln, 8 Lower Cross Cottages, Udimore, Rye, East Sussex TN31 6AT, **490**

Takada, Suguru, Yokohama-Shi, Naka-Ku, Suehiro-Cho 1-2-3, Iseichi Bldg 2F, 231-0046, Japan, **784**

Talbot, Kate, 1 Dover Place, Bristol, Somerset BS8 1AL, **530**

TAPIES, Antoni, Hon RA, The Artist, c/o Waddington Galleries, 11 Cork Street, London W1S 3LT, **11**

Tauber, Lucy, 63 Wilton Way, London E8 1BG, **936**

Team Shampoo, c/o Kostas Grigoriadis, Flat 9 Galaxy House, 32 Leonard Street, London EC2A 4LX, **929**

Teasdale, Anna, 121 Catherine Way, Batheaston, Bath, Somerset BA1 7PB, **319**

Theobald, David Edwin, 18 Ellesmere Road, Twickenham TW1 2DL, **1091**

Thomas, Amy, Castle Naze Farm, Combs, High Peak, Derbyshire SK23 9UX, **551**

Thomas, Guy, 9 St Johns Road, Lower Weston, Bath, Somerset BA1 3BN, **1019**

Thomas, Lex, Dalston Underground Studios, 28 Shacklewell Lane, London E8 2EZ, **340**

Thompson, Kathleen, 3 Haynes Cottages, High Street, Brasted, Westerham, Kent TN16 1HS, **943, 972**

Thompson, Liam, Stone Cottage, Hogbens Hill, Selling,
Faversham, Kent ME13 9QU, **442**

TILSON, Joe, RA, Courtesy of Waddington Galleries,
11 Cork Street, London W1S 3LT, **626, 642, 644**,
Courtesy of Alan Cristea Gallery, 31 Cork Street,
London W1S 3NU, **256, 261, 267**

Tim Lucas, Price & Myers LLP, 30 Newman Street, London
W1T 1LT, **899**

Tindall, Susan, 171 Woodlands Way, Southwater,
Horsham, West Sussex RH13 9DS, **325**

TINDLE, Dr David, RA, c/o Redfern Gallery, 20 Cork Street,
London W1S 3HL, **1154, 1175, 1176, 1177, 1185, 1192**

Tinsley, Francis, 28 Ewell Court Avenue, Epsom, Surrey
KT19 0DZ, **103, 534**

Tong, Kurt, 66 Gainsborough Road, Richmond TW9 2EA,
1034

Tonkin, Paul, 30 The Gardens, East Dulwich, London
SE22 9QF, **991**

Traberg, Carina, 14 Marlborough Road, London N19 4NB,
1048

Trayte, Jonathan, Studio 11A, c/o AB Fine Art Foundry,
1 Fawe Street, London E14 6PD, **159, 268**

Treby, Janet, Lodge Cottage, West End, Kingham,
Chipping Norton, Oxfordshire OX7 6YL, **295**

Tsolakis, Elena, 53 Hackney Road, London E2 7NX, **806,
848**

TUCKER, William, RA, c/o Gallery Pangolin, 9 Chalford
Ind. Estate, Chalford, Gloucestershire GL6 8NT, **48**

Turk, Gavin, 31 Museum Street, London WC1A 1LH, **1045**

Turner, Annie, 111B Brookbank Road, London SE13 7BZ,
650, 765

Turpin, Louis, 19 Udimore Road, Rye, East Sussex
TN31 7DS, **476**

Turvey, Simon, 2 York Rise, Orpington, Kent BR6 8PR,
466

TWOMBLY, Cy, Hon RA, Courtesy of The Eli and Edythe
L. Broad Collection, Los Angeles, USA, **574**

U

Umerle, Julie, Flat 10, Seacon Tower, 5 Hutchings Street, London E14 8JX, **745**

Underwood, George, 90 Priory Road, London N8 7EY, **1119**

Ungureanu, Florin Catalin, 10 Dominic Court, 43 The Gardens, London SE22 9QR, **338**

Unsworth, Jim, 14 Manor Lane, London SE13 5QP, **563**

Urbanek, Maciej, 71 Manor Avenue, London SE4 1TD, **1057**

V

Velasco, Jazmin, 6 Tile Kiln Lane, London N6 5LG, **140**

Verity, Charlotte, 8 Love Walk, London SE5 8AD, **294**

Vibert, Elizabeth, 71 Lower Redland Road, Bristol BS6 6SP, **302**

Vickery, Ben, HOK Sport Architecture, Unit 14 Blades Court, 121 Deodar Road, London SW15 2NU, **820**

von Haselberg, Martin, 1125 5th Avenue, New York, NY 10128, USA, **1257**

W

Wagstaff, Lee, c/o Rise Berlin, Hertzberg Str. 27, Berlin 12055, Germany, **76**

Waldron, Dylan, 2 Hallaton Road, Slawston, Nr Market Harborough, Leicestershire LE16 7UA, **411**

Walker, Stuart, 3W Architecture, Thames Wharf Studios, London W6 9HA, **906**

Walker Bushe Architects, 6 Highbury Corner, Highbury Crescent, London N5 1RD, **816**

Walsh, Nicky, Flat 5, Springfield House, Lettsom Street, London SE5 8JY, **1064**

Walter, Stephen, 96 Margaret Road, New Barnet, Hertfordshire EN4 9RB, **108, 1058**

Ward, Ann, Suggate House, 49 Quay Street, Halesworth, Suffolk IP19 8EY, **519**

Ward, Jane, 66 Mayall Rd, London SE24 0PJ, **1023**

Ward, Michael, Flat 85, Pinehurst Court, 1–3 Colville Gardens, London W11 2BJ, **211**

Wardle, Adam, 48 Beaconsfield Road, London N15 4SJ, **375**

Warnants, Ceal, 47 Omega Works, 4 Roach Road, London
E3 2PD, **75**

Warner, Zheni, 187 Newmarket Road, Norwich, Norfolk
NR4 6AP, **979**

Warrillow, David, 18 Botanic Crescent, Glasgow G20 8QJ,
Scotland, **485**

Watanabe, Noriko, 38A Randolph Avenue, London
W9 1BE, **32, 729**

Watson, Grant, 131 Hartington Road, London SW8 2EY,
706, 707

WEARING, Gillian, RA, Courtesy of Maureen Paley,
21 Herald Street, London E2 6JT, **1059**

Wells, Robert, 2 Ruskin Road, Eastbourne, East Sussex
BN20 9AY, **313**

Westerhof, Tisna, 44 Musgrove Road, London SE14 5PW,
560

Weston Williamson, 43 Tanner Street, London SE1 3PL,
854

Whale, Sue, 22 Forester Road, Bath, Somerset BA2 6QE,
97

Whicheloe, Oscar, Chalfont, Hillbrow Road, Esher,
Surrey KT10 9UD, **471, 482**

WHISHAW, Anthony, RA, 7A Albert Place, Victoria Road,
London W8 5PD, **613, 615, 616, 947, 948, 978**

White, Donna, 84 Portlock Road, Maidenhead,
Berkshire SL6 6DZ, **1007**

White, Michael B, 143 Old Church Street, London
SW3 6EB, **495**

White, Victoria, 46 Starfield Road, London W12 9SW,
1036

White Table, c/o Felicity Atekpe, White Table, Unit 5B,
20-30 Wilds Rents, London SE1 4QG, **790**

Whittlesea, Michael, Flat 98, Defoe House, Barbican,
London EC2Y 8ND, **316, 497**

Wickham, Joceline, 293 Dereham Road, Norwich,
Norfolk NR2 3TH, **457**

Wiener, Jenny, Flat, 5 Deanery Street, London W1K 1AZ,
172

WILDING, Alison, RA, Courtesy of Karsten Schubert,
5–8 Lower John Street, London W1F 9DR, **666**
Wilkins, Ingrid, 48 Lyndale Avenue, London NW2 2QA,
510
WILKINSON, Chris, OBE RA, Wilkinson Eyre Architects,
24 Britton Street, London EC1M 5UA, **891, 907**
Williams, Annie, 31 Ellington Street, London N7 8PN,
352
Williams, Charles, 21 Warneford Street, London E9 7NG,
1121, 1122
Williams, Dominic, Ellis Williams Architects, Chester
Road, Preston Brook, Runcorn, Cheshire WA7 3BA,
862
Williams, Evelyn, 12 Finsbury Park Road, London N4 2JZ,
1166, 1167
Williams, Thomas, 77 Lupin Point, Abbey Street, London
SE1 2DW, **135**
Williamson, Joby, 36 Maynard Road, London E17 9JG,
210
Wilson, Arthur, 22 Wingate Road, London W6 0UR,
732
Wilson, Martin, 88 Hilliard Road, Northwood,
Middlesex HA6 1SW, **1038**
WILSON, Richard, RA, 44 Banyard Road, London SE16
2YA, **645, 647, 876, 1266**
Wincer, Richard, 4 Beechwood View, Oakville Road,
Hebden Bridge, West Yorkshire HX7 6NR, **98, 164**
Winder-Boyle, Ann, PO Box 975, Beaconsfield,
Buckinghamshire HP9 1ZA, **533**
Winkelman, Joseph, 69 Old High Street, Headington,
Oxford OX3 9HT, **379**
Woodall, David, The Studio, Upper Court Road,
Woldingham, Caterham, Surrey CR3 7BF, **522**
Woodley, Gary, Upper Flat, 10 Cricketfield Road, London
E5 8NS, **776**
WOODROW, Bill, RA, Courtesy of Waddington Galleries,
11 Cork Street, London W1S 3LT, **663, 671**, c/o Royal
Academy of Arts, **667, 668, 669, 670**

Wragg, Gary, c/o Flowers East, 82 Kingsland Road, London E2 8DP, **730, 1005**
WRAGG, John, RA, 6 Castle Lane, Devizes, Wiltshire SN10 1HJ, **2, 3, 1113, 1157**
Wright, Lisa, Chapel House, Crelly, Helston, Cornwall TR13 0EY, **974**
Wright, Simon, 41 Melton Road, Wymondham, Norfolk NR18 0DB, **317**
Wright, William, Basement Flat, 33A Corinne Road, London N19 5EZ, **555**
Wylie, Rose, 30 The Street , Newnham, Sittingbourne, Kent ME9 0LQ, **700, 939**

X

Xin Yu, SABE, University of Westminster, 35 Marylebone Road, London NW1 5LS, **810**

Y

Yuasa, Katsutoshi, Cite Internationale des Arts, Atelier 8409, 18 Rue de l'Hotel de Ville, Paris 75180, France, **79, 85**

Z

Zeschin, Elizabeth, Hurston Studio, Hurston Lane, Pulborough, West Sussex RH20 2EW, **1033**

SUPPORTING THE ROYAL ACADEMY

Supporting the Royal Academy

The Royal Academy of Arts receives no annual government funding and is entirely reliant on self-generated income and charitable support. Registered Charity No. 212798

The Royal Academy Trust

Registered Charity No. 1067270

The Royal Academy Trust was founded in 1981 to receive, invest and disburse funds given in support of the Royal Academy of Arts. Since then the Trust has raised an endowment fund which now amounts to nearly £23 million, the income from which helps to finance the Academy's charitable activities, and has obtained funding totalling almost £60 million for capital projects, including the creation of the Sackler Wing. The recent phase of works included the restoration of and improvements to the Main Galleries, the Annenberg Courtyard and the John Madejski Fine Rooms, now open to the public for exhibitions from the newly catalogued and conserved Royal Academy Permanent Collection.

Become a Patron

The Royal Academy's Patron Groups form a vital source of income in the absence of public funding. The Patron Groups maintain and develop the Academy's internationally renowned exhibition programme; fund education projects for children, families and people with special needs; provide scholarships and bursaries for art students in the RA Schools; and help to conserve the Academy's unique Permanent Collection.

Further information on charitable giving to the Royal Academy may be obtained from Ian Vallance, Head of Patrons and Friends, on 020 7300 5624 or from Caitlin Coen, American Associates of the Royal Academy Trust, 555 Madison Avenue, Suite 1300, New York, NY 10022, USA.

Leaving a Legacy to the Royal Academy

Leaving a legacy to the Royal Academy is perhaps the most personal way to make a lasting contribution to its future. By including the Royal Academy in your Will, you can commemorate the inspiration and enjoyment which the Academy has given you over the years and help to ensure that it continues to enrich people's lives for generations to come.

For more information about leaving a legacy to the Royal Academy, please call Reema Khan, Deputy Director, Regular Giving, on 020 7300 5666 for confidential advice.

Corporate Opportunities

Since its foundation in 1768, the Academy has remained both independent and self-supporting, receiving no government funding for the annual exhibitions or education programmes. The Academy has been successfully leading the fields of arts sponsorship, corporate membership and corporate entertaining for the past 25 years.

Together, these aspects make a significant financial contribution, enabling the Academy to maintain both the excellent artistic reputation for which it is known and its home, Burlington House, and to fulfil the role it plays in the cultural life of this country.

Since 1979, the Academy has worked with over 180 sponsors across a broad range of areas including exhibitions, education, fundraising events and the Royal Academy Schools. The Corporate Development team also looks after 80 corporate members who enjoy numerous benefits for their staff, clients and community partners.

Sponsorship and corporate membership can offer companies:
- Priority booking and exclusive entertaining in the Royal Academy's suite of eighteenth-century Fine Rooms and contemporary space at 6 Burlington Gardens, for business presentations, breakfasts or dinners, combined with Private Views of exhibitions
- Comprehensive crediting on all publicity material and involvement with press and promotions campaigns (sponsorship only)
- Invitations to prestigious Royal Academy corporate and social events
- Special passes for unlimited entry to all Royal Academy exhibitions
- Free entry for employees; behind-the-scenes tours; lectures and workshops for staff and their families
- Regular monitoring and evaluation
- A dedicated team of experienced staff to manage every aspect of sponsorship, corporate membership and corporate entertaining.

Further details are available from the Corporate Development Office on 020 7300 5620/5709.

Royal Academy Trust

Registered Charity No. 1067270

American Associates of the Royal Academy Trust

Japanese Committee of Honour

Mr Tadao Suzuki *(Chairman)*
and Mrs Suzuki

Corporate Members	
Mr Kunio Anzai (Tokyo Gas Co., Ltd) and Mrs Anzai	Mr Hideo Morita (Morita Asset Management Co., Ltd) and Mrs Morita
Mr Yoshiharu Fukuhara (Shiseido Co., Ltd) and Mrs Fukuhara	Mr Takeo Obayashi (Obayashi Corporation) and Mrs Obayashi
Mr Nobuyuki Idei (Sony Corporation) and Mrs Idei	Mr Nobutada Saji (Suntor Limited) and Mrs Saji
Mr Yoshitoshi Kitajima (Dai Nippon Printing Co., Ltd) and Mrs Kitajima	Mr Soichiro Shimizu
Mr Yoshihiko Miyauchi (ORIX Corporation) and Mrs Miyauchi	Mr Toichi Takenaka (Takenaka Corporation) and Mrs Takenaka
Mr Yuzaburo Mogi (Kikkoman Corporation) and Mrs Mogi	Mr Shoichiro Toyoda (Toyota Motor Corp.) and Mrs Toyoda
Mr Minoru Mori HON CBE (Mori Building Co., Ltd) and Mrs Mori	Mr Yuzo Yagi (Yagi Tsusho Ltd) and Mrs Yagi

Patrons	
Prof Tadao Ando HON RA and Mrs Ando	Mr Masayoshi Son and Mrs Son
Mr Akito Arima and Mrs Arima	Mr Jonathan Stone and Mrs Stone
Mr Sanji Arisawa and Mrs Arisawa	Mr Hideya Taida HON CBE and Mrs Taida
Mr Hiroaki Fujii and Mrs Fujii	Mrs Michi Takahashi
Mr Shinji Fukukawa and Mrs Fukukawa	Mr Shuji Takashina and Mrs Takashina
Mrs Hisako Hatakeyama	Mr Tsuneharu Takeda and Mrs Takeda
Mr Hirotaro Higuchi and Mrs Higuchi	Mr Hiroyasu Tomita and Mrs Tomita
Prof Arata Isozaki HON RA and Mrs Isozaki	Mrs Yasuko Yamazaki
Mr Yohji Shimizu and Mrs Shimizu	Mrs Yu Serizawa *(Director)*

Royal Academy Supporters

The Trustees of the Royal Academy Trust are grateful to all of its donors for their continued loyalty and generosity. They would like to extend their thanks to all of those who have made a significant commitment, past and present, to the galleries, the exhibitions, the conservation of the Permanent Collection, the Library collections, the Royal Academy Schools, the education programme and other specific appeals.

Patrons of the Royal Academy Trust

In recent years the Royal Academy has established several Patrons Groups to encourage the regular and committed support of individuals who believe in the Royal Academy's mission to promote the widest possible understanding and enjoyment of the visual arts.

The Royal Academy is delighted to thank all its Patrons for generously supporting the following areas over the past year: exhibitions, education, the Royal Academy Schools, the Permanent Collection and Library, Anglo-American initiatives and for assisting in the general upkeep of the Academy, with donations of £1,250 and more.

Royal Academy Patrons

Benefactor Patrons

Benjamin West Group Patrons

Silver Patrons	Wendy Becker Payton	Lady Judge
	Mrs Adrian Bowden	Scott and Christine Morrissey
	Mr and Mrs Paul Collins	Mr and Mrs John R Olsen
	Kim Dunn	Frank and Anne Sixt
	Charles and Kaaren Hale	

Bronze Patrons	Ms Ruth Anderson	Ms Theresa A Parker
	Mrs Alan Artus	Lady Purves
	Tom and Diane Berger	Mr and Mrs K M Rubie
	Wendy Brooks and Tim Medland	Sylvia Scheuer
	Debra Cajrati Crivelli	Mr and Mrs Thomas Schoch
	Mr and Mrs Gunnar L Engstrom	Carole Turner Record
	Mrs Clare Flanagan	Frederick and Kathryn Uhde
	Cyril and Christine Freedman	Mr and Mrs Ullmo
	Mr Andrew Hawkins	Mr John D Winter
	Suzanne and Michael Johnson	Mary Wolridge
	Charles G Lubar	
	Mr and Mrs Patrick Mahon	*and others who wish*
	Neil Osborn and Holly Smith	*to remain anonymous*

Schools Patrons Group

Chairman	John Entwistle OBE DL

Platinum Patrons	Matthew and Sian Westerman

Gold Patrons	Mr and Mrs Paul Myners

Silver Patrons	Lord and Lady Aldington	Philip Marsden
	John Entwistle OBE DL	

Bronze Patrons	Mrs Inge Borg Scott	Peter Rice
	Ian and Tessa Ferguson	Anthony and Sally Salz
	Prof Ken Howard RA	Mr Ray Treen
	and Mrs Howard	*and others who wish*
	Julia Fuller	*to remain anonymous*

Contemporary Patrons Group

Chairman	Susie Allen

Patrons

Tarek Aguizy
Mrs Alan Artus
Viscountess Bridgeman
Dr Elaine C Buck
Miss Camilla Bullus
Jenny Christensson
Gus Danowski
Helen and Colin David
Belinda de Gaudemar
Chris and Angie Drake
Lissa Engle
Ms Soma Ghosh
Elizabeth Griffith
Mrs Selma Gürtler
Caroline Hansberry
Mrs Susan Hayden

Penelope Mather
Mary Moore Danowski
Angela Nikolakopoulou
Barbara Pansadoro
Mr Andres Recoder and Mrs
    Isabelle Schiavi
Richard and Susan Shoylekov
John Tackaberry
Inna Vainshtock
Dr Yvonne von Egidy-Winkler
Lawton Wehle Fitt
Cathy Wills
Mary Wolridge

*and others who wish
to remain anonymous*

Trusts and Foundations

The Atlas Fund
The Ove Arup Foundation
Aurelius Charitable Trust
The Peter Boizot Foundation
The Bomonty Charitable Trust
The Charlotte Bonham-Carter
    Charitable Trust
William Brake Charitable Trust
The Britten-Pears Foundation
R M Burton 1998 Charitable Trust
C H K Charities Limited
P H G Cadbury Charitable Trust
The Carew Pole Charitable Trust
The Carlton House Charitable
    Trust
The Clore Duffield Foundation
The Coexist Foundation
John S Cohen Foundation
The Ernest Cook Trust
The Sidney and Elizabeth Corob
    Charitable Trust
The Coutts Charitable Trust
Alan Cristea Gallery

The de Laszlo Foundation
The D'Oyly Carte Charitable Trust
The Dovehouse Trust
The Gilbert and Eileen Edgar
    Foundation
The Eranda Foundation
Lucy Mary Ewing Charitable Trust
The Fenton Arts Trust
The Margery Fish Charity
The Flow Foundation
Gatsby Charitable Foundation
Goethe Institut London
The Golden Bottle Trust
The Great Britain Sasakawa
    Foundation
Sue Hammerson Charitable
    Trust G
The Charles Hayward Foundation
The Hellenic Foundation
Heritage Lottery Fund
A D Hill 1985 Discretionary
    Settlement
The Harold Hyam Wingate

Foundation
Institut fuer
Auslandsbeziehungen e.V.
The Japan Foundation
Stanley Thomas Johnson
Foundation
The Emmanuel Kaye Foundation
The Kindersley Foundation
The Kobler Trust
Lapada Association of Art &
Antique Dealers
Lark Trust
The David Lean Foundation
The Leche Trust
A G Leventis Foundation
The Leverhulme Trust
The Lynn Foundation
The Maccabaeans
The McCorquodale Charitable Trust
Mactaggart Third Fund
The Simon Marks Charitable Trust
The Marsh Christian Trust
Martineau Family Charity
The Paul Mellon Centre
The Paul Mellon Estate
The Mercers' Company
Margaret and Richard Merrell
Foundation
The Millichope Foundation
The Henry Moore Foundation
The Mulberry Trust
The National Manuscripts
Conservation Trust
The J Y Nelson Charitable Trust
Newby Trust Limited
OAK Foundation Denmark
The Old Broad Street Charity Trust
The Peacock Charitable Trust
The Pennycress Trust
PF Charitable Trust
The Stanley Picker Charitable Trust
The Pidem Fund

The Edith & Ferdinand Porjes
Charitable Trust
The Fletcher Priest Trust
The Privy Purse Charitable Trust
Pro Helvetia
Mr and Mrs J A Pye's Charitable
Settlement
The Radcliffe Trust
Rayne Foundation
T Rippon & Sons (Holdings) Ltd
The Rose Foundation
Schroder Charity Trust
The Sellars Charitable Trust
The Archie Sherman Charitable
Trust
The South Square Trust
Spencer Charitable Trust
Stanley Foundation Limited
Oliver Stanley Charitable Trust
The Steel Charitable Trust
Peter Storrs Trust
Strand Parishes Trust
The Joseph Strong Frazer Trust
The Swan Trust
Swiss Cultural Fund in Britain
Thaw Charitable Trust
Sir Jules Thorn Charitable Trust
Tiffany & Co
Tillotson Bradbery Charitable Trust
The Albert Van den Bergh
Charitable Trust
The Bruce Wake Charity
Celia Walker Art Foundation
Warburg Pincus International LLC
Weinstock Fund
Wilkinson Eyre Architects
The Spencer Wills Trust
The Maurice Wohl Foundation
The Wolfson Foundation
The Hazel M Wood Charitable Trust
The Worshipful Company of
Painter-Stainers

American Associates of the Royal Academy Trust

Friends of the Royal Academy

Patron: HRH The Duke of Edinburgh KG KT
Chairman: Ron Zeghibe

Visit free all year round
Explore the art of all periods and cultures
Make the most of the RA
Become a Friend today...

- Free entry
- No ticket queues
- Visit as often as you like
- Bring a family adult guest and up to four family children free
- Relax in the Friends Rooms
- See each exhibition first at previews
- Receive the quarterly *RA Magazine*
- Participate in events and tours

... all from just £70 a year *

Join the friends
at the RA Friends desk in the front hall
by post: Friends Office
                   Royal Academy of Arts
                   FREEPOST 33 WD 1057
                   Piccadilly
                   London W1E 6YZ
by facsimile: RA Friends, 020 7300 8023
                   (but not if paying by direct debit)
by telephone: ring 020 7300 5664 with your
                   credit card details
visit us at www.royalacademy.org.uk/friends

* prices valid until 31 March 2010

Royal Academy Corporate Membership Scheme

Launched in 1988, the Royal Academy's Corporate Membership Scheme has proved highly successful. Corporate Membership offers company benefits to staff, clients and community partners and access to the Academy's facilities and resources. The outstanding support we receive from companies via the scheme is vital to the continuing success of the Academy and we thank all members for their valuable support and continued enthusiasm.

Premier Level Members	
Accenture	Goldman Sachs International
The Arts Club	Hay Group
A T Kearney	HSBC plc
Bain Capital	JTI
The Bank of New York Mellon	Kleinwort Benson Private Bank
Barclay's plc	LECG Ltd
Booz & Company	Lombard Odier Darier Hentsch
CB Richard Ellis	Northern Trust
Deutsche Bank AG	Schroders plc
Ernst & Young LLP	Smith and Williamson
GlaxoSmithKline plc	Standard Chartered

Corporate Members	
All Nippon Airways	Denton Wilde Sapte
Apax Partners	Diageo plc
Arcadia Group plc	Doll
BGC Brokers L P	F & C Asset Management plc
BNP Paribas	GAM
The Boston Consulting Group	Heidrick & Struggles
Bovis Lend Lease Limited	Insight Investment
British American Business Inc.	ITV plc
British American Tobacco	John Lewis Partnership
Calyon	JP Morgan
Canon	KPMG
Capital International Limited	Lazard
Christie's	London College of Fashion
Citi	Man Group plc
Clifford Chance	Mizuho International plc
Concateno Plc	Momart Limited
Control Risk Group	Morgan Stanley
Curzon Partnership LLP	Navigant Consulting

Registered Company No. 2216104

Nedrailways
Novo Nordisk
Osborne Samuel LLP
Pentland Group plc
Rio Tinto
The Royal Society of Chemistry
Skadden, Arps, Slate, Meagher &
   Flom

Slaughter and May
Société Générale
Timothy Sammons Ltd
Trowers & Hamlins
Veredus Executive Resourcing
Weil, Gotschal & Manges
Windsor Partners

Sponsors of Past Exhibitions

The President and Council of the Royal Academy would like to thank the following sponsors and benefactors for their generous support of major exhibitions during the last ten years:

ABNAMRO
Akkök Group of Companies
American Associates of the Royal
     Academy Trust
American Express
A T Kearney
Aygaz
Bank of America
The Bank of New York Mellon
Barclays
BBC Radio 3
BNP Paribas
British American Tobacco
Canon
Cantor Fitzgerald
Carlsberg UK Ltd
Castello di Reschio
Chase Fleming Asset Management
Christie's
Classic FM
Corus
J F Costopoulos Foundation
Country Life
Cox & Kings
Credit Suisse First Boston
The Daily Telegraph
Danske Bank
Guy Dawson
Debenhams Retail plc
Deutsche Bank AG
Diageo plc
E.ON
Ernst & Young
Eurohypo AG

Eyestorm
Farrow & Ball
Fidelity Foundation
Lucy Flemming McGrath
Foster + Partners
Game International Limited
Garanti Bank
The Gatsby Charitable Foundation
The Jacqueline and Michael Gee
     Charitable Trust
GlaxoSmithKline
Goldman Sachs International
The Great Britain Sasakawa
     Foundation
Guardian
The Hellenic Foundation
Ibstock Building Products Ltd
The Independent
Insight Investment
International Asset Management
The Japan Foundation
JTI
Donald and Jeanne Kahn
Lassa Tyres
A G Leventis Foundation
Harvey and Allison McGrath
Mercedes-Benz
Merrill Lynch
Mexico Tourism Board
Mizuho International plc
Stavros Niarchos Foundation
Novo Nordisk
OAK Foundation Denmark
Pemex

	RA Exhibition Patrons Group	Time Out
	Reed Elsevier plc	UBS Wealth Management
	Virginia and Simon Robertson	Walker Morris
	The Royal Bank of Scotland	Yakult UK Ltd
	Sotheby's	
Other Sponsors (sponsors of events, publications and other items in the past five years)	Carlisle Group plc	Martin Krajewski
	Country Life	Marks & Spencer
	Derwent Valley Holdings plc	Michael Hopkins & Partners
	Dresdner Kleinwort Wasserstein	Morgan Stanley Dean Witter
	Goldman Sachs International	Prada
	Gome International	Radisson Edwardian Hotels
	Gucci Group	Richard and Ruth Rogers
	Hines	Rob van Helden
	IBJ International plc	The Wine Studio
	John Doyle Construction	

Royal Academy Schools

The Royal Academy Schools provide the only three-year postgraduate course in Fine Art in the United Kingdom. The criteria for acceptance are positive commitment and a convincing potential for creative development. This is a small, exceptional school with a challenging atmosphere of experimentation and strong sense of identity.

The Schools attract a comprehensive range of visiting tutors, both practitioners and theorists, and there exists within the studios an ongoing atmosphere of critical debate and forward-looking enquiry.

The traditional forms of painting, sculpture and printmaking are pursued alongside newer media such as digital printing in a state-of-the-art Epson suite, and facilities for photography and video.

There are no fees and students are assisted financially in a limited way by means of a variety of awards, prizes and travel bursaries.

The Schools' central London location and close proximity to the remarkable international standard exhibition programme of the Royal Academy in Burlington House greatly enhance the rich cultural and educational environment that exists here.

RASA (Royal Academy Schools Alumni) is the association of current and past students of the Royal Academy Schools.

Chairman: George Waud
Co-chairman/Administrator:
  Gloria Steemsonne

Membership Secretary:
  Hilary Frew
Contact: 020 7300 5715

Library

The Library of the Royal Academy is for the use
of its Members, staff and students, and is open for
specialist research by appointment.

Telephone: 020 7300 5737
e-mail: library@royalacademy.org.uk

AGBI

Artists' General Benevolent Institution
Burlington House
Piccadilly
London W1J 0BB

Patron: HRH The Prince of Wales

Founded in 1814 by JMW Turner, the AGBI provides help to professional artists and their dependants in time of trouble.

Funds are always needed and donations of any amount are gratefully received and acknowledged. Cheques should be sent to The Secretary at the above address.

Registered Charity No. 212667
Contact: 020 7734 1193